PLAIN SELLING

SELLING IS SIMPLE BUT NOT EASY

DAVID YULE

ISBN: 0957515723
ISBN-13: 9780957515727

I first wrote Emotional Selling in the late 1990's. 87 Tips for Practical Selling was published in 2005. A lot has changed since then. Research is being conducted all the time that throws up new ways of thinking.

The concepts in the first 2 books still remain valid but I needed to bring them up to date. Some duplication is therefore inevitable. I have improved the way I teach the concepts and have made them more practical. I have found examples that aid understanding. I use industries that I have worked with to explain how the concepts apply. I am sure they apply to you, in your culture, in your industry and with your prospects.

My sales training methods are used all over the world and there is a proven record of success.

I am always happy to receive feedback and discuss any area of selling so please feel free to get in touch.

David Yule

david@gtiuk.com

TABLE OF CONTENTS

PLAIN SELLING

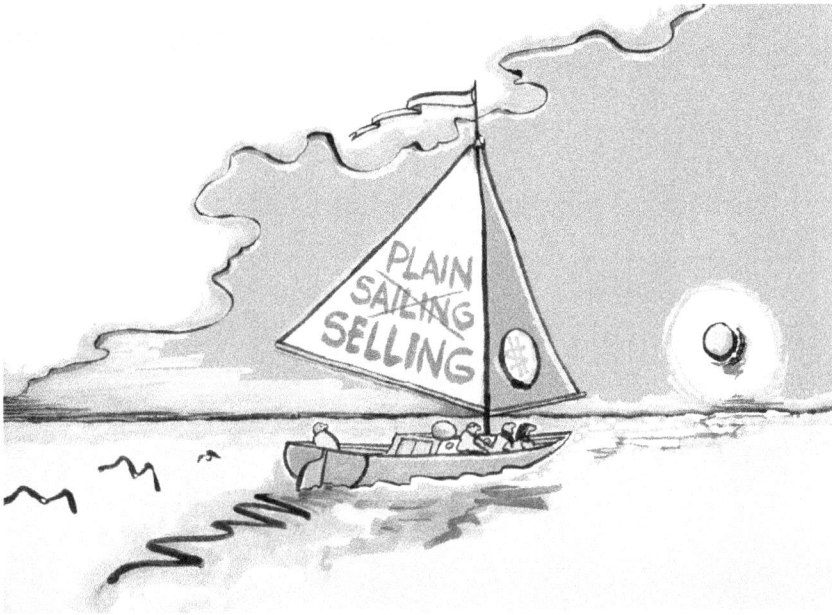

A NEW APPROACH

80% of all decisions are made emotionally. I believe people make purchasing decisions emotionally and then justify their decision to themselves and others logically. Logic plays very little part in the decision making process.

If you are in any way like me I am sure you have made a purchase that wasn't wise. Maybe you bought an item of clothing, a book, a bicycle or sportswear etc. For me it is usually a gadget! Many times I have thought this purchase will enhance my life in some way only to discover that I never use the product. I certainly never used it in the way I thought I would (I have used a book to prop up a table)!

Selling is not a perfect science. If you do all the 'right' things it doesn't mean you will get a sale. If you do all the 'wrong' things you won't necessarily lose a sale.

I am writing this book for people who want to improve their selling skills. They may be looking for a job in selling or they may just have landed a selling role. They may have been in a selling role for many years and just changed jobs. They may have been in selling for longer than they care to remember and been on more courses than Tiger Woods. They just know they can do, and want to do, better.

I am writing it because no matter how much you have learned it isn't the full story.

How does this book differ from other selling books?

- It comes from no 'right' perspective

- It challenges basic beliefs about selling

Because I believe that decisions are made emotionally I am not trying to work out why things happen, merely explain that they do happen.

The book has been organised into three sections:

In section 1 I deal with the myths of selling and some psychological factors that affect everyone, salespeople, customers and prospects.

Section 2 deals with considering prospects as individuals with different motivational needs.

Section 3 looks at the skills and attitudes that help to make salespeople successful.

So let us start with some selling myths:

SECTION ONE

'PSYCHOLOGICAL' FACTORS FACING BUYERS

MYTHS ⊙F SELLING

Open and Closed Questions

My litmus test of a sales trainer is their attitude towards 'open' questions. First of all let me give some definitions of 'open' and 'closed' questions, any of the follow may apply:

Open Questions

Cannot be answered by 'yes' or 'no' e.g. 'tell me about your order process?'

Seek to get opinions as opposed to factual information e.g. 'what do you think about .....?'

Try to get the prospect to give more than one or two word answers e.g. 'can you elaborate on that for me?'

They are answered by more than a few words irrespective of the question e.g. the salesperson asks 'do you want a red one or a blue one' and the prospect answers by going into a long monologue about the merits of either colour!

Closed Questions

Can be answered by 'yes' or 'no' e.g. 'do you want to go ahead?'

Seek to get factual information as opposed to opinions e.g. 'tell me about your order process?'

Try to get the prospect to give a one or two word answer e.g. 'is that acceptable to you?'

They are answered by a few words irrespective of the question e.g. the salesperson asks 'what style are you thinking about' and the prospect answers 'we don't know'.

I can tell you categorically I have never been able to find any empirical evidence that supports the view that if you ask more 'open' questions you will be more successful. There have been many studies that have found there is absolutely no correlation between 'open' and 'closed' questions and your success as a salesperson.

One excellent study showed no correlation with success whatever definitions of open and closed questioning are used. It was a study of telephone selling which has a major advantage. In telephone selling you can record the entire conversations easily. Repeated playbacks can ensure certainty in categorising questions accurately as open or closed. You can also change the definitions and run the statistical analysis again.

The researchers considered more than 50,000 telephone calls and found no correlation between 'open' and 'closed' questions and success. They found this irrespective of what definitions were used.

So why do sales trainers persist in teaching 'open' and 'closed' questioning techniques? It is mainly because logic tells them that it should be important. It is probably also because they are not aware of the research on questioning.

Salespeople treat prospects as individuals

I would often ask salespeople, 'why don't you treat these prospects as individuals?' The salespersons answer was that they thought they did. I would record how many times salespeople would interrupt, whether they would give opinions, whether they would ask opinion or fact questions. Whether they varied their pitch to appeal to the type of person. How they attempted to handle objections etc. I am sad to report that there seems to be little variation within a salesperson and much variation between salespeople. By this I mean that salespeople tend to interrupt based on the salespersons own personality not the prospects. If the salesperson liked the sound of their own voice they would talk a lot irrespective of the prospect. Their 'pitch' and 'objection handling' became remarkably repetitive, almost as if they were reading from a script.

So why do they do that? We define service in our own terms. We decide what is good service as far as we are concerned and treat everybody the way that we would like to be treated. It was from this discovery that I started to use my behaviour model, which I will explain later. The point of this is to get salespeople to vary their style based on the behaviour style of the prospect and gives tips on how to do so.

Men and Women are the same!

I know this isn't really a myth! It's not that men and women are the same, the myth is that they want to be treated the same. In selling we often get this very wrong.

Women wanted to be treated equally with men but not identically to them. Now bear in mind that studies have shown females to be the decision maker in up to 80% of all consumer purchases!

Some major factors that differ:

In tests more men perform better at 3D space awareness tests such as the one shown below. These are the tests where you see a cube with shapes on each side that has been flattened. The test involves mentally rearranging the shape to predict what it will look like when it is assembled as a cube. The impact of this is when you are showing plans (say of a bathroom) to women most will have difficulty with constructing an image of what the finished room would look like. This explains the success in 3D design programmes which are a must for successful selling today.

3D Space awareness test

Imagine the following puzzle was made of cardboard. When you fold the top shape which of the following cubes is the correct one?

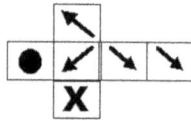

In general if you ask a man to describe their life, they talk of achievements (job title, trophies won etc.) Females generally describe their life in terms of relationships (partner, children etc.) In selling relationships seem to be more important to females and they expect more time to be spent developing them before transacting business together. Females seem to take a longer term view.

Studies have shown that the average woman, throughout the world, says between 12-14,000 words per day. The average man says between 8-10,000 words. Match the communication style of your prospect.

Tests show that women are more multi-tasked whereas men are more mono-tasked. When reading a man will switch 95% of his hearing off. He may still retain listening for 'attentive' words such as his name. When a male prospect is reading don't speak!

(The correct answer to the 3D space awareness test is 'A')

Scripted Selling is BAD!

Somehow we are frightened of scripted selling. You know the type of thing. Someone calls you and sounds like they are reading a script. You give an answer and you can sense they are looking at their crib sheet for the appropriate response. This is bad selling not scripted selling.

You wouldn't pay to go and see many plays in the theatre when they are doing the first read through. The power of theatre or film is when they are following a script, word for word, and they make it sound like it is an impromptu speech. The best ad-libs are practiced to death.

We use scripts endlessly, answering the telephone, greeting friends, etc. In selling we also use scripts although for the most part they are informal and not written down. If you are using scripts you may as well write them down and check that they are a good script! Then you should learn the script so that it sounds natural.

Knowledge equals implementation

I am a sales trainer. I sometimes feel that companies want to wheel me in to do a training session and if the delegates know what they should be doing then they will do it. It doesn't work that way. Major behavioural change takes a lot of effort and happens slowly. It takes continuous redirection and reinforcement. Learning styles have to be taken into account. Changing attitude is a slow process. Habits, even good habits, are hard to break.

Prospects know what they want and need

In my experience most prospects:

Don't know what they want

Don't know what they need

What they want and what they need are different.

The myth is that you can just walk into a prospect's office and question them about their needs to sell to them. It is far more complex than that.

Interestingly, I ask on courses, 'why do people buy things' the most popular answers are:

They need it

Or

They want it

Neither of these is true and I can prove it. Most salespeople sell more of what they like. In fact in the same showroom side by side can be two salespeople, one selling more of one product and the other selling more of a different product. Where did prospect needs or wants come into this equation?

Prospects are more knowledgeable today than they have ever been

They may have more information now. This will often be called the information age but will never be referred to as the knowledge age. More information just means more conflicting information. Take any election; I am sure I have more information from the parties than my grandfather had. Which biased information should I believe?

Prospects certainly play the negotiating game better than they ever have. Prospects certainly often research on the internet before talking to salespeople and may appear to have more knowledge.

The truth is the world is so complex today that it is becoming more important to consult specialists. Where we had monopolies they have been replaced by confuse-opolies where companies make things more complex in order to exploit the complexity.

The abundance of choice means that it is impossible to do any meaningful comparisons. I researched in a supermarket and discovered more than eighty different types of milk! From full fat, skimmed, semi skimmed, evaporated, soya all the way to milk specifically for cats!

Information does not equal knowledge.

Positive thinking is the key to sales success

Positive thinking isn't nearly as effective as positive action. Opportunity is often disguised as hard work, which is why so many people miss it.

I am intrigued by a perceived sea change in professional sportsmen. I was watching the British Open golf recently and interviewees were playing down expectations rather than using the positive thinking psychobabble of the past. They can all think positively and still only one will win.

We will look at this in more detail in the section headed 'Attitude'.

Salespeople need to know about competitor's products.

It may help some salespeople. I found that it leads to salespeople disagreeing with prospects in a way that meant they could never win. For example if the prospect said the competitors product did something that was unique in the salespersons product the salesperson would try to, tactfully, inform the prospect of their error!

What I learned as I got older was that proving people wrong wasn't a good sales tactic! I also learned if the prospect thought the competitor's product would do something it didn't then that probably meant the prospect didn't use that feature.

For example imagine I was selling a radio that had AM and FM. The prospect told me their current radio had AM and FM when **I knew** it only had FM. I could pretty well guarantee that the prospect couldn't see the need to listen to AM radio. If they did then they would know that their current radio didn't have that facility. My job would then be to highlight the need for AM. If you can't convince that there is a need or want then there won't be a sale anyway.

I found that focussing on my own products and my own strengths I was more successful. I can hear people saying how would you know your strengths unless you research competitor's products? I am not saying the company shouldn't know competitor's weaknesses I am saying they needn't be known by the salesperson. The best way for salespeople to find the strengths of their own products is to ask existing loyal customers why they buy them.

People don't buy features they buy the benefits

If that is true how come they sell mountain bikes in the Netherlands?

Very few people can explain what a graphic equalizer does. In the event of your graphics falling behind does it help them catch up? Obviously it wouldn't ever allow your graphics to get ahead and win the race!

There are some people who buy features. Equally there are some people that avoid too many features, which I will deal with later when we look at Professional Buyers.

My research also shows there is a line beyond which benefits become a liability. We will look at this in the section on Differentiation.

Objections are opportunities

If that is the case why don't you start creating some objections in order to make sure you have an opportunity?

The only reason there are salespeople is to handle objections. There would be no reason to spend all that money on salespeople if there were no objections. I am amazed when interviewing potential salespeople, i.e. people that have never sold before. One question I ask is 'what would you like to sell and what wouldn't you sell?' It is amazing how many people answer this by saying they want to sell something worthwhile that is good value for the prospect and wouldn't like to sell something that isn't good value. I feel they are really saying they want to sell something that sells itself!

Objections are best avoided and if you can't avoid them learn to deal with them.

It helps to find out why people don't buy from you

It helps much more to find out why people do buy from you.

The reason for this is that people buy emotionally and justify logically. If you are asking why people didn't buy from you they will only give logical reasons. These are just throwing you off track.

I always wondered why salespeople listened more to people who didn't buy rather than people who did. I sold products that everyone loved.

For the most part we only ever got two objections; 'I don't have the need' or 'it's too expensive'. I wondered why our salespeople always fought for reducing our prices. They had greater belief in the word of people who didn't buy rather than the word of people who knew they were expensive and thought they were worth it.

The best way to teach salespeople is to give them a sales process

I know processes are important in business. Large businesses couldn't function well without them and, as Buckingham & Coffman found in First Break All The Rules, a process may prevent failure but it won't ensure success either.

For me the sales process is obvious and usually followed (although sometimes not very well)!

The process I teach:

Avoid Objections

End of.

The Sales Process that is usually followed is:

There is some form of INTRODUCTION	-	Maybe not done well
There is an attempt to ESTABLISH A NEED	-	Possibly not brilliantly
There is PRESENTING THE CASE	-	Evidence may be dodgy

There is a call to ACTION   -   Not   always   because
                                                  sometimes   it   is
                                                  inappropriate!

If you want I can easily make this more complex!

The role of a salesperson is to avoid or handle objections that may occur at any time in this process.

All the rest is designed to make sales trainers look clever (probably fails)!

I don't need to teach salespeople not to ask for the business before they have introduced themselves. I may have some value in helping them to understand the importance of establishing credibility or explaining some of the psychological factors in persuasion.

A last introductory thought; if you are not having fun you aren't selling as much as you could.

So let's get on with how we go about this great profession.

AVOIDING OBJECTIONS

Objections come in all shapes and sizes. They happen at all stages. Some objections you handle before they happen some you didn't anticipate and so they happen before you can avoid them.

Many objections are not really objections. For example 'is that your best price?' That is a question not an objection. The answer should be, or at least it should imply, 'yes it is'. I believe that people know quality costs more and they are prepared to pay for quality and they don't want to be ripped off. Prospects do ask for a fair price, they want to know if anyone else gets a lower price and most are not seeking to get something for nothing.

If I am asked for my best price I often use humour. For example I am selling something for £300 and I am asked if it is my best price. I respond 'No, I could do it for £400 but it is best for me unfortunately'. You would be amazed how often this works.

For the most part it is better to handle objections before they occur. For example sales people tell the prospect of the benefits of a product in order to handle a price objection. We build up the value of the product so the prospect sees the price value equation as a positive and therefore they don't object when you give them the price.

This book is almost exclusively about handling objections before they occur.

Before going further though I want to look at some well-established psychological principles that may help or hinder our quest to maximise sales effectiveness.

PSYCHOLOGICAL PRINCIPLES

Some psychological pressures that affect the behaviour of people generally.

Confirmation Bias

I am always intrigued when participants on a training course say to me 'Why do people ask us for a discount and the same people don't ask check out operators in a Tesco supermarket for a discount?'

The answer to me is self-evident. Somehow they are conveying to the prospect that it is appropriate to ask them for a discount. Tesco convey the message to customers that it would be a waste of their time to ask for a discount.

Let's look at how salespeople transfer the information that prospects should ask for a discount.

First of all I would like you to answer a question. 'How important do you think price is in the decision to buy?' That is, relative to the other things which are important in the decision to buy?

How would you rate it on a scale of 0% to 100%, where 0% is absolutely irrelevant up to 100% it is the only thing that is important?

Let me give you a clue here – no one should write down 100%. If price was 100% of the decision to buy then people would walk into shops and say, 'Here is my £100, what can you give me that is cheap'? The product wouldn't matter. There must be some other things that are more important than the price, such as the product. What I am asking is, relatively speaking, how important is price?

Before you answer this I should give you some idea of my thoughts:

> It is probably different for different people. Give an average for your prospects.

> It is probably different for retail and business-to-business (B2B). If you work in more than one give separate answers.

> It is probably different depending on the value of what you are selling.

> It is probably different based on how much competition is around you.

> There are probably cultural differences and industry differences.

> There is no right answer; I am just looking for a rough answer and am asking you to think about your belief. It should be about your prospects in your type of business.

Note your answer.

Confirmation Bias is:

> *'A tendency to actively seek evidence that proves what we already believe to be true and to ignore evidence that contradicts our beliefs'*

So depending on your answer I can predict whether customers ask you for a discount. What I found when studying salespeople is that some people get lots of customers asking for a discount yet others get very few requests. The factor that correlates with this is your beliefs about how important price is in the decision to buy.

Earlier, I explained that salespeople sell to prospects the way that the salesperson would like to be sold to. The same thing happens with price. If the salesperson believes price is important in the decision to buy then the natural way for them to sell would be to focus on overcoming the price to value equation.

Let me show you the impact of Confirmation Bias. Suppose I asked you:

'What questions would you ask someone to find out if they are religious?'

On some courses I have been asked:

'What do you do on a Sunday?'

'Do you believe in God?'

'Do you read the Bible?'

'Do you pray?'

'Do you observe religious festivals?'

On other courses I get asked:

'What do you do on a Friday?'

'Do you believe in Allah?'

'Do you read the Koran?'

'How many times a day do you pray?'

'Do you observe Ramadan?'

You can probably see what is happening. The first answers come from courses in the UK or other Christian countries. The second questions come from my work in the Middle East.

No one has ever asked me 'Do you worship the devil?'

In other words we ask questions from a positive, not a negative, perspective. We also betray our own beliefs by the questions we ask. So when a salesperson believes that price is important they betray their beliefs by asking questions from a positive perspective.

When you understand Confirmation Bias my experience with a client makes sense.

About 10 years ago I started working with a client outside of Scotland (my own culture). When I started the training retail salespeople would tell me I didn't understand their culture. They said, 'Maybe people in Scotland don't ask for a discount but everyone in our country asks for a discount'. They told me that their media encouraged prospects to negotiate and it was impossible to survive in their business without discounting. Almost 100% of their sales involved a discount.

Today they rarely discount and last year when I was working with the same company I asked a group of relatively new salespeople: 'how often do prospects ask for a discount'? The answer was 'very rarely'. Either we have changed the culture of the entire country (and I don't think I am that good!) or we have changed the way people sell. We have changed the way people in the company sell and it is almost entirely down to Confirmation Bias.

Don't get me wrong, prospects still ask, 'is that your best price?' and the salespeople have been taught to deal with that. They use an implied statement, 'yes, that is our competitive market price'. This implies that the price has already been discounted and this method handles the question 99% of the time.

In fact people are actually suspicious of low prices and discounts.

This has recently been supported by a study with rail passengers. It was found that no one on a train thinks they got the lowest fare available for their journey. Even the people who did get the lowest fare!

There have been several studies that found that prospects that receive a negotiated discount are generally less happy with a purchase transaction than people who asked for a discount and were refused. How can that be?

I believe the reason for this can be explained by 'buyer's' remorse'.

Buyer's Remorse

Car manufacturers did a study to find out if it was worth spending huge amounts of money on car brochures. They discovered something that amazed them.

They found a category of people that read car brochures almost from start to finish. Have a guess about who that would be? Car nuts? Nerds? No certainly not. The people that read a brochure from start to finish are ….. those who have just bought a car! Brochures are read after the purchase not before.

Here is what happens.

We buy a car; get home with a receipt having paid a lot of money. The receipt doesn't look like £10,000's worth so we read the brochure to convince ourselves that we have done the right thing. So 'buyer's remorse' kicks in as soon as we have committed to a purchase, especially an expensive one.

It makes me think that most companies should do more work on post-purchase consolidation. For example homebuilders could have a champagne party for new purchasers in their show home. The buyer could invite all of their friends to see their great new purchase. The advantage of doing this is that you could reduce deposits in the knowledge that cancellations would reduce. Handing over a deposit has a big downside in the commitment process. Make it easier for people to buy and they will buy more.

How does 'buyer's remorse' account for unhappiness when you get a discount? After you make a purchase two things are going through your head:

- Could I have got more discount if I negotiated harder?

- Is the thing I have just bought really worth what I have paid for it?

If you ask for a discount and are refused there is a reassurance that no matter how hard someone negotiates they will still pay the same as you. It also implies that what you are paying is the real value.

So if you understand Confirmation Bias I can now explain why prospects ask you for a discount. You tell them to ask you for a discount. You do this because of your beliefs.

If you go back to the figure you put down earlier let me make some comments.

Some of the problems I get on courses are because of maths, and I understand that. I hear lots of people claiming to give 110% effort. Unfortunately the decision to buy is 100%. Price is one aspect of this; everything else needs to be divided into the remainder.

On courses I will often get people saying that price is 80% of the decision to buy. I then ask that person a series of questions. Here are some typical answers:

How important is product quality?   90%

How important is stock availability?   80%

How important is location?   90%

How important is service?   100%

How important is after-sales?   90%

How important is the brand?   90%

And they think price is   90%!

We are now up to 620% of the decision to buy!!!!

If you accept that the things mentioned above are more important than price then the answers would be:

How important is product quality?   15%

How important is stock availability?   15%

How important is location?   15%

How important is service?   15%

How important is after-sales?   15%

How important is the brand?   15%

How important is the price?   10%

Total   100%

We know that there are things more important than price. It is easy to work this out, if you don't change the price but change other things you can then measure their impact on sales. It shows whether they are more important than the price. In other words if you reduce the quality of the product and retain or reduce the price and sales drop then product quality must be more important than price.

All of the following things are more important than price. The evidence in no particular order:

Peer Group Pressure

Big companies are usually more expensive than small companies. The biggest lawyers, accountants, plumbers, carpenters, builders, manufacturers and telephone companies are all the most expensive. The biggest company is usually the most expensive. If price was the most important thing you would need to be the least expensive to become the biggest.

Product Quality

If you reduce the product quality the sales will go down even if you keep the price the same.

Stock Availability

If you have no stock sales go down (you can't sell what you don't have!)

Location

If you build a new store the sales in that area will go up, if not why on earth are Tesco investing so much money building new stores.

Relationship

The vast majority of business is conducted with people we have done business with before. Generally the most profitable business in a company is from loyal prospects. When my sales team said 'but boss the competition are cheaper' I would reply 'that's why we employ you! If we were cheaper as well we wouldn't need you'.

After-Sales

If you deal with after-sales poorly, people are disloyal irrespective of prices.

Environment

Even the paint on a showroom wall is more important than price! If not why would any company refurbish their showroom? When you give the showroom a facelift the sales increase. The big shopping centres also look the most luxurious.

Brand

The brand is more important than the price. Gerald Ratner can explain that! He made an off-the-cuff remark about the quality or rather lack of quality of their products and almost killed the brand. Even reducing the prices couldn't stop the sales from falling.

FedEx decided to compete on price, it was a disaster and they ended up losing $29 million. Success came when they changed their focus to, 'When it absolutely, positively has to be there overnight'.

Apple has 70% of the tablet market – Samsung has less than 10%. Which one is less expensive?

Packaging

The box the product comes in is more important that the price. In one company I worked with we sourced our biggest selling product locally instead of from the USA and the colour of the product packaging changed. The sales dropped. They only picked up again when the sales team caused such a stir that we went back to the old packaging.

The evidence that the packaging is more important than the price is easy to find. Take any of your products bash up the box a bit and put it right next to a pristine box. No one will want the beat up box. You will have to lower the price to sell it.

Sales Ability

The skill of the salesperson is more important than the price. If you have two salespeople in the same location with the same prices, stock, brand etc. the best salesperson will achieve better sales and margins.

The first page of Google will do more for your sales than your prices.

So does your website and the ease of getting around it. An interesting point about Google, did you know the Page ranking mentioned on a Google search started because the founder of Google (Larry Page) gave the page a ranking! The ranking carries his name.

Opening hours

Corner shops generally charge more and they open longer. Perhaps this is one of the reasons that the big stores are opening longer. Taxis charge more at night.

Waiting Time

My daughter went to Disneyland and proudly told me of a pass that she bought which meant they didn't have to queue for the rides. These priority passes were restricted (scarcity sells) otherwise most would buy them rather than waiting and they would end up waiting in a priority queue!

I asked her how much the passes cost and even immediately after her holiday she had no idea. Spending hours waiting in a queue with a four-year-old is not her idea of a holiday.

People pay extra for next day delivery. They will even pay retailers in the UK extra to know whether the delivery will be in the morning or afternoon.

Habit

Several studies have shown that habit is the biggest buying motivator; we don't change suppliers lightly.

Consistent Pricing

When working with trade suppliers we found that customers needed consistent pricing rather than low pricing. They charge their customers based on what they were charged by their supplier. The customers systems couldn't cope with prices changing on a day-to-day basis or changing depending on which branch they bought the goods from.

As a consumer inconsistent pricing angers me. It is annoying to get on a train paying different fares from last week. I guess it hurts me more when this week is less expensive than last week! I now think I was overcharged last week and there is nothing I can do about it.

Marks and Spencer have changed their complaints policy. If you buy something and take it back for a refund they will only refund the lowest price they have sold the item for, not the amount paid. I guess this is a flawed attempt to stop people exposing their inconsistent pricing. Customers buy something, then see it at a lower price in a sale, and take it back for a refund so they can buy it again, at the lower price. An illustration might make that clearer!

You buy a shirt for £30 then see it in their sale priced at £15. You take it back for a refund hoping for £30 refund so you can buy it again for £15 and take advantage of the sale price. The policy of refunding the lowest price it was sold at means you would only get a refund of £15. It seems, to them, they have solved this problem. The unintended consequence is they have annoyed the many genuine customers (to cater for the exceptional customers) who now only get a refund of £15.

So these fifteen things (and I am sure I have missed some out) are more important than the price in the decision to buy.

If I now go back to the question' how important is price in the decision to buy?' We have fifteen things that, on the basis of the evidence, are more important in the decision to buy than price. Even if these fifteen were all exactly equal, the absolute maximum figure for the price would be 6%.

I rarely meet any salesperson (and I was the same until someone taught me) that doesn't massively overstate the importance of price in the decision to buy. If you answered that price is less than 6% of the decision to buy you may want to skip the rest of this section because it is aimed at the people who believe that price is more important than it is.

The problem is Confirmation Bias predicts two things:

1.) There is a belief persistence and in spite of all the evidence the chances are you will be ignoring the evidence and finding your own evidence to support your beliefs.

2.) Your questions are being shaped by your beliefs and if you believe price is important then you transfer that belief to your prospects and hence they will ask you for a discount.

IGNORING THE EVIDENCE

One of the things you may be saying to yourself is, 'That may be right for retail but it isn't right for trade'. So the next question is, 'Do you think retail or trade is more price sensitive?'

On courses I would say at least 90% of people think trade is more price sensitive. This doesn't make sense to me. Business-to-Business sales must be more service sensitive. I believe neither is really price sensitive but retail is very slightly more sensitive than trade.

Here is the evidence:

Businesses lose money from poor service

If a delivery is delayed a retail prospect will get annoyed but generally they don't lose money. If you are waiting for your new washing machine to be delivered and it doesn't come it will be an inconvenience.

If Ford motor company are waiting for a delivery of starter motors and they have to stop a production line until they get a delivery they could lose millions.

I learned this lesson quite early in my career when our company sold electronic components. I took a telephone call from a prospect asking if we had a certain component in stock. We had 10 of them in stock. He said he wanted to order three and would collect them. I said: 'I am sorry, when I said in stock I meant in our warehouse in Phoenix.' He said, 'Yes, I know, I would like you to make sure they are ready for collection in the USA. As soon as your warehouse opens, they will be collected.'

I proceeded with the order and followed our policy: 'Would you like me to confirm the price?' The customer got very annoyed and said 'I have a production line down waiting on this part. It is costing me £250,000 per hour. I am getting the part collected in Arizona and someone will fly with the part so that it isn't stopped at customs. Do you think I care about the price? You are wasting my time!'

You only have to look at the difference between a shop and a business trade counter. Pop in to your local kitchen showroom. If no one speaks to you for 20 minutes you will probably be relieved that you haven't been annoyed by a salesperson. No one would wait 20 minutes at a trade counter. How long do people spend wandering around in B&Q compared with time spent in Screwfix?

How long does it take a company to deliver your kitchen? Two weeks wouldn't be uncommon. How long does it take someone to deliver car parts to a trader? 30 minutes isn't uncommon.

Businesses lose money from poor quality
If your car breaks down you get annoyed and it is inconvenient, you may decide not to buy that type of car again but usually you don't lose money. If a product fails it can be catastrophic for a manufacturer. They lose money. They may get some compensation from the supplier but there is no way that would compensate for the damage to their brand.

So much so that many manufacturers spend millions testing products from 3rd party suppliers. Product quality far outweighs price. To prevent a purchasing department getting too focused on price most businesses have a design or technical department to specify the quality level way before price even becomes a consideration.

Businesses don't even pay the price

Businesses pass the price they pay on to their prospects. If a pub decides to stock a more expensive brand of vodka, they don't pay the difference; they merely increase the price of that vodka to their prospect.

In fact, because most businesses work on percentages, if their price is higher they make more profit. If you are buying something for £1000 and adding on 30% mark up then your profit is £300. If the price goes up to £1100 you now make £330. I will cover this in the negotiation section as well because the opposite normally happens when you reduce your price.

Business class flights are more expensive than economy class.

Businesses are concerned with making profit. If they think a lower price will help them make more profit then of course they are concerned about the price. Most businesses suffer the cost of poor service and poor quality; they can't charge their prospect for the poor service they have received but they can pass on the cost of good service and good quality.

Remember businesses can charge your price on to their prospect but it is hard for them to charge the time they waste looking for a better price. Think of it this way; a carpenter will make more money building cabinets than they would shopping for lower prices. They are carpenters, not professional buyers.

So your belief persistence may lead you down the wrong path. Your first instinct may be 'I can see that this is right for others but it isn't right for my business'. Price is relatively unimportant in virtually all businesses. Except of course high prices! That is how you create a premium brand. So when I say price is relatively unimportant I mean low prices.

Let's go back to your questions, which are shaped by your beliefs. The same prospects that ask you for a discount don't ask Tesco for a discount and so it strikes me the problem cannot be blamed on the prospect.

The reasons people ask you for a discount are because of the way you sell and the messages you give.

Which brings me to the worst questions in selling: 'What is your budget?' or 'How much have you been quoted?' — indeed any question that effectively sets you up for a negotiation.

The reasons this is the worst thing you can say are:

- Does anyone tell the truth when answering? Can you rely on their answer?

- Does anyone spend less than their budget?

- People don't decide budgets - they form them. If you were going to look for a new garden shed, chances are you wouldn't start saving; you would go out to find out how much it is going to cost you to get what you want.

- There is a better way – 'Top Down Selling' where you present ranges from the most expensive to the least expensive rather than starting with the basic model and working up.

So how do you get prospects into the frame of mind that makes it more likely they will ask you for a discount? It is because of what we, as salespeople, say.

Have you ever said anything like:
- 'You'd better sit down before I give you the price'

- 'The best I can do is'

Do you use phrases that encourage the prospect towards negotiation?
- 'How does that sound?'

- 'You are our biggest prospect'

- 'You know we value your custom'

- 'You have been a customer for a long time and we don't want to lose you'

- 'We really want to do more sales with your business, in this area etc.'

Do you use phrases that invite the prospects to challenge?
- 'Comparatively speaking, I think you will find that we are the best price on this'

- 'Our new reduced prices are .....'

- 'Our price is lower than anybody's'

Do you use phrases that change you from a salesperson to a satisfier?
- 'Tell me where I need to be?'

- 'What do I have to do to win your business?'

- 'Am I in the ballpark?'

- 'Would you be willing to pay xxx for this?'

- 'I can always give you a better price if .....'

- 'If you get a better price come back to me'

If prospects frequently challenge you on price you have probably been working at handling price objections rather than avoiding price objections.

I have already stated I believe price is relatively unimportant in the decision to buy. Because of my beliefs and the operation of 'Confirmation Bias' I seek evidence that proves that price is relatively unimportant. My entire sales training career has been based on helping others to understand the evidence.

You may have been collecting evidence that price is important. If so, let's consider where you are probably collecting the evidence:

- From prospect's?

- From people that don't buy from you?

- From your own shopping habits?

- From the media which seems to promote low prices as a way to succeed?

Let's examine these in more detail:

From prospects

I believe money is not a real motivator but it is a perceived motivator. Consider an employee with a bad attitude who is underperforming.

If you pay them more would they agree to perform better? Pay them more and within a few weeks you will now have a slightly richer employee with a bad attitude still underperforming! So money is a perceived motivator and doesn't actually motivate in the long-term.

There is another way this manifests itself. When real motivation is absent people complain, not about the real motivator, but about the perceived motivator.

So when you are failing to motivate employees the most likely thing that people start complaining about is their salary. Happy employees don't look for other jobs! If employees are complaining about salaries, look elsewhere for the reasons for their demotivation.

Customers are exactly the same as employees. Extremely loyal customers rarely complain about pricing.

When you service a customer badly or fail to deal with a complaint properly customers will complain about your prices.

From people that don't buy from you

I have already mentioned that salespeople seem to place more emphasis on people that don't buy from them. In fact I even found some of my salespeople seemed to believe that in some way the people who were paying our prices were uninformed. Customers didn't seem to know they could get the same thing for a lower price.

Yet almost every business is approached, daily, by salespeople promising to save money. In fact to approach someone with the purpose of saving them money isn't a particularly successful way of getting business. How do you react when someone telephones your house saying they can save you money?

When a proposal is turned down prospects normally blame something they think you have no control over. I call it the 'Politeness Principle'.

People will say:

- 'Your price was too high'

- 'Your product lacked some features'

- 'Your location is wrong'

- 'We needed something you couldn't provide'

People will not say 'I did not buy it from you because I don't trust you'! Yet we know we buy from people we trust.

From your own shopping habits
Do you buy on price? Chances are you think you shop around; most people do. Shopping around doesn't mean you buy on price; what, where, how and why have to be considered.

Think about these questions:

- What computer or mobile phone do you have? I am amazed at how many people tell me they buy on price whilst checking email on their iPhone!

- What car do you have?

- Who is your mobile phone provider?

- Have a look at your watch; what brand is it? What is the cheapest watch you have in your bedside cabinet?

- Do you (or your partner) shop in Aldi, Lidl or Tesco?

- What trainers do your children wear?

- Have you seen how much a Louis Vuitton handbag costs? Now compare the salary of the people who buy these handbags to your salary!

- Do you have low price Sky TV, Fox Sports or do you just watch Free to View?

- Would you prefer to shop in John Lewis or the 'cheapy' shop in town?

- What golf clubs do you play with?

- Every day you probably get bombarded with emails and phone calls offering you a better price on mobile phones, utilities and insurance. How much time do you allow for the person on the other end of the phone? A few seconds delay when you pick up the phone tells me it is a cold call. Many friends simply replace the phone when that happens.

- Which of these builders' quotes would you accept?

  - Quote 1   £10,000

  - Quote 2   £11,000

  - Quote 3   £ 1,860

Do you really buy on price or is that a perception?

From the media

It seems that wherever you look the way to succeed is through low prices.

Everywhere you are bombarded by low prices. Every High Street shop has a sale on. I can buy a colour television for just over £100 even though when they were first launched in the early 1960s I think they were £300!

Does anyone think the DFS (UK), or Harvey Norman (Australia) sale will end soon?

Greed is a big motivator. 'Free' is still the most powerful marketing word.

Promotions everywhere: www.myvouchercodes.com can give you special offers.

There is a difference between the perception of price being important and the reality.

We no longer have monopolies there are only confuse-opolies. Confuse-opolies are companies that are making their pricing structure so complex that no one can understand them and price comparisons are impossible. Try checking out the lowest priced mobile phone deal and you will see what I mean. Are you on the 'best' tariff for your electricity and gas? Would you know if you were?

Surely Amazon's success is down to low prices? Amazon is a great story. Sure they started their business selling books at lower prices than the traditional outlets. They broke a cartel and getting a reputation for low prices was easy.

Are they a low price organisation? Is their success down to low price? I buy lots of things from Amazon. I do it because it is easy, they are open 24 hours, they have a great returns policy and I can buy with a very good safety net. Not because they are cheap. In fact I don't think they are. I recently received a delivery from Amazon with a note from the seller that said if I order direct from them next time they would offer me a 5% discount. I still order through Amazon. They have also recently been ordered to change their terms and conditions for sellers, which were anti-competitive. They tried to insist that sellers didn't offer to sell at a lower price than they did on Amazon. That is illegal.

If you look for a product on Amazon, copy the part number and Google it to find it cheaper, normally you will find the only place you can buy that product is Amazon. A tactic that many companies use today is to use their own part numbers. It makes it very difficult to compare prices because you don't know if you are comparing the same product.

Companies that fail should be a good indicator of how important price is. Look at the high priced companies: how many have failed? Have you ever known a company with high prices to fail? If you can think of an example (and I can't) remember to ask yourself did they fail because their prices were high or because they were poor companies?

How about low price companies that fail? I can reel off Courts Furniture, MFI, Hygena, Woolworths, Land of Leather, Allied Carpets, Kwik Save and Peacocks. I am sure if I put my mind to it I could think of many more.

Confirmation Bias always affects you. It affects everyone. Even being aware of its existence does not change the effect. It will affect you. The only question that you can choose your answer to is: 'How will it affect you?'

You have a choice to let Confirmation Bias affect you positively or negatively. Assuming you had a figure of more than 6% in the question about the importance of price above your choices are:

Continue to believe that price is important in the decision to buy

or

Decide that price is relatively unimportant and learn the skills of showing the prospect the value of what you do.

I believe my competitive position is entirely in my area of concern. How competitive I am depends on how efficiently I run my business but it depends much more on other businesses. What I charge doesn't make me competitive; it is what others charge that is important. If it is in my area of concern I should ignore it and focus on things I can control such as my skills, my communication and my attitude.

As a salesperson do you think it is more constructive to believe that price is important knowing that there will always be someone else cheaper? Or, is it more constructive to believe that the real drivers of success are service, quality, relationships, brand, environment etc.?

In order to stop transferring the message to prospects that price is important the first thing you have to do is believe price is not important yourself. This is the first way to avoid a price objection.

When you have done this

Stop asking prospects why they didn't buy from you (it will only make you feel bad!)

Stop blaming price for losing business. Instead of saying 'we lost it because we were too expensive' start saying 'we lost it because the prospect cannot see the value of what we do. How can we get better at showing the value of what we do?'

When you and your product are perfect, when you did everything absolutely right, when no one could possibly have done better than you then maybe, just maybe, you could think about blaming the price.

Start going to loyal prospects and ask them why they buy from you? These are your unique selling points, the real differences between you and others. Reinforce them with prospects. Sell them using all the techniques that influence prospects.

Look for the evidence that supports your new belief.

In looking at 'Confirmation Bias' I have given examples where price affects the behaviour of the salesperson and that isn't always the case. Confirmation Bias will affect you whether you think about beliefs in terms of Price, Brands, Product Quality, Service and all sorts of other areas.

A great example of 'Confirmation Bias' is a business that sold almost exclusively to the trade. They decided to broaden their business and opened a showroom where they could sell direct to the public. The problem was that the salespeople had convinced themselves, and subsequently the managers, that people coming into the showroom were simply 'time wasters'. They wanted to look but didn't want to buy.

What do you think a business with that sort of 'Confirmation Bias' would do? What they did was lock the showroom door and put up a sign stating entrance by appointment only! That would weed out the timewasters wouldn't it? Trouble was it weeded out everyone!

Another example was a business that convinced themselves that Trade sales were more price sensitive than retail sales. What would they do? They proved they were right by pricing everything lower for retail prospects! Of course they made less profit from retail. They then changed their mind and put up their retail prices and now make higher margins from the retail side. They should now convince themselves that they were right all along and put up the trade prices again!

I was asked to coach the sales team of an international training company. I am paraphrasing but this is the essence of what happened. One salesperson went to a prospect that wanted team building training. The salesperson questioned them on their needs and convinced the prospect that in fact they needed time management training, because poor time management was causing the team relationship problems.

Same coaching contract, another prospect and a different salesperson – this time the prospect wanted time management training. Following the questioning the solution they came to was? You've guessed it; this time the solution was team building! The salesperson convinced them the relationship problems were causing the time management pressure.

One customer thought they needed team building training but bought time management. The other thought they needed time management but bought team building!

On both occasions the final solution may have been the right one – there is no way to tell. Both prospects bought the suggested solution and there wasn't a way that I could measure the success of the training. I can't help feeling that the 'Confirmation Bias' of the two salespeople influenced the solution.

Now that you understand 'Confirmation Bias' remember that it applies to both sides. You are affected and so is your prospect. This means if the prospect believes something and you confirm it then the prospect will most likely accept your evidence. If the prospect has a contrary belief to you then they will most likely discard your evidence.

This makes the process of avoiding objections tricky if you don't understand the beliefs of your prospect. Logic isn't a good persuader because prospects discard logic if it doesn't support their beliefs

When we look at avoiding and handling objections it is always important to bear this in mind. We need to avoid emotional objections as well as avoiding logical objections.

It is worth repeating that Confirmation Bias states that we will seek to prove what we already believe to be true and ignore evidence to the contrary.

Shortcuts

Because of the sheer amount of information available people use mental shortcuts to make decisions. It is almost impossible to analyse every single decision to the nth degree. Studies have shown that the average adult makes in excess of 30,000 decisions in a day. These decisions range from 'where will I sit?', 'will I brush my teeth now or later?', to ones that will have an important and lasting impact.

How can we possibly analyse all the available choices with so many decisions to make? We can't so we follow shortcuts. Psychologists call these Heuristics.

For example imagine you want two bottles of wine, one for everyday and one for a special event. What shortcuts would you most likely use to decide on quality? Many studies have shown the principle indicator you would use is the price. You will, in all probability, pay more for the 'special' bottle. Incidentally in blind taste tests there are absolutely no correlations between the taste and the price of wine.

We use brands to decide quality. We use the look of the bottle to decide whether we will like the liquid inside it. We think if airline toilets are clean the engines are probably well maintained.

When avoiding or handling objections we need to be aware of the shortcuts the prospect will use. They can be the difference between the prospect accepting and rejecting your proposal.

Authority

We think experts are more trustworthy than laypeople. Someone in a uniform is more likely to be trusted. People are more likely to give change to someone in a uniform for a parking meter etc.

This credibility is amplified if someone other than you announces it. For example imagine you wanted a team building training course and the trainer explains that they have been conducting team building training for many leading organisations for over 10 years. Do you think that would have the same effect as a receptionist saying, 'I'll put you through to Mary who has been conducting team building training for many leading organisations for over 10 years'? It turns out the receptionist is much more powerful even though they clearly have a vested interest in your acceptance of the expertise.

Physiotherapists are able to persuade clients to go on a diet and stick to a diet for longer if they simply display their credentials on the wall of the treatment room. The certificates you have earned for attending training courses do have an impact!

In handling or avoiding objections we will need to use words and techniques that give credibility to our role as 'experts'.

Conformity

To have a society you must have conformity. You can't have some people driving on the left and others driving on the right! Conformity is instilled in us from a very young age and is a very powerful force.

Almost everyone goes in buildings through doors marked 'Entrance' and out using doors marked 'Exit'.

It causes us to behave in some automatic ways also. For example when we enter a showroom (in countries where we drive on the left) we turn left and go round clockwise. We avoid people so if someone is sitting at a desk immediately on the left then we will turn right but feel uncomfortable about it. We would spend less time in this showroom than if there aren't salespeople blocking our flow.

We will allow people to control our movements in our place of business. For example we can lead someone around taking them from one side of a showroom to another. This even works in trade counters and other places of work. It can also work when you are in their premises.

People will follow an agenda if we use one. We can explain to people that they need to give us information because it is standard business practice.

We can get people to touch things, turn things on and off, play with things when you tell them to do so. All it needs for this to work is you acting as if everyone did it.

Use an overview of the process you will follow when you meet a new prospect. It turns out prospects are happier if they know the process, in advance. Tell everyone your normal way of doing business when you meet them.

Part of conformity is our need to take turns in conversations. If you watch a new mother with her child you will see them taking turns from a very early age. Mummy says goo goo ga ga or it may be ga ga goo goo for all I know and then waits for the baby to repeat. This turn taking stays with us throughout our life.

This explains the success of what I call the 'one second rule' Psychologists have discovered that in a conversation there are generally no periods of complete silence for over one second. This is why people say ehm. What they are really saying is, it is still my turn, please don't interrupt while I gather my thoughts.

If someone speaks to you and you don't answer within one second they will generally go on to supply more information. The second thing they will say is more likely to be more truthful and accurate than the first thing.

When teaching salespeople this rule many have difficulty at first. Remember I am not saying stay silent for the rest of your life simply for less than one second!

If you watch carefully we send signals when we want to speak:

• Perhaps an audible inhalation

• Maybe leaning forward

• Move our hands

We also may give signals that we think it is the other persons turn:

- We may stop talking!

- May raise our eyebrows

- Nod

- Sit back

Learn to use short periods of silence to encourage others to speak.

Consistency

People prefer to be seen as consistent.

Imagine you wanted people to put up a big, ugly sign in their garden campaigning for a village bypass. How can you improve the success ratio of resident's acceptance? The way to do is by using consistency. You ask people to put a small inoffensive sign in their window first. A study showed that people who have put the small sign in their window were four times more likely to agree to the larger sign in the garden.

As a general rule this means that we don't have to establish credibility. If we are there then we must have credibility. Imagine if you won the lottery. How many financial advisors would you invite to deliver a presentation on what they could do for you? Usually people ask three potential advisers to make a presentation. How many would you invite that you think aren't professional or are dishonest?

The problem with establishing credibility is neatly summed up by Shakespeare:

'The lady doth protest too much, methinks'.

Establishing credibility actually does the opposite. Assume credibility – you wouldn't be considered if you weren't credible.

How can you tell if a prospect is interested in buying your product? Their lips move! When they aren't interested in a product they won't ask questions. It would be inconsistent to say 'I hate that product but what is it made of?'

Consistency can be used to avoid objections by asking questions before prices are discussed. For example:

- 'Do you look for quality products or cheap products?'

- 'Do you prefer products that last or are you happy with cheaper products?'

Asking customers what they think during a sale is a way to avoid 'I need to think about it' at the end. It would be inconsistent of them to keep saying what they think and then use 'I need to think about it' as an objection.

From little acorns big oak trees grow. If you have never sold to a prospect before try going for a small sale first rather than pitching for a big contract. It would be inconsistent to place even a small order with a company you don't trust.

Peer Pressure

People like to feel they are doing things that other people do as well. A neat experiment will serve to show the principle.

You have probably seen little signs in a hotel saying that the hotel owners care about the environment and asking if you would reuse towels. What if the sign said 80% of people **in this hotel** reuse their towels? Would there be a difference if the sign said 80% of people **in this room** have reused their towels?

As you may expect the sign saying 'in this room' gets a far bigger reuse ratio.

Reciprocation

Human beings have a need to reciprocate. It is generally felt that it is impossible to have a society unless there is a need to reciprocate. We can't live together unless we can do things knowing we won't, always, be exploited.

In an experiment a person working in an office was asked to treat colleagues in two ways:

To one side of the office they were asked to be very helpful, getting coffee, helping with filing and doing errands etc. generally to be thoughtful and helpful.

To the other side they were asked to be polite and friendly and if they were asked for help to make an excuse and avoid helping.

At the end of the week the person was asked to sell raffle tickets and you can guess which side bought more.

This is useful to us in that our need to reciprocate increases with the strength of what the person does for us. i.e. how difficult it was for them to do the task. If someone smiles at us we need to reciprocate and smile back and if we really put ourselves out people feel they 'owe us something'.

Giving someone a brochure isn't as powerful as taking a picture of an item that you print out and give to the person. Getting someone else to take the picture is even more powerful.

The need to reciprocate is why doing things 'without obligation' still leaves most people feeling obligated. Notice that it doesn't make everyone feel obliged. There are always some people who don't conform.

Just because some people are dishonest doesn't mean we should treat everyone as if they were. When using reciprocation, for example, if I give someone a drawing or plan of my design they may still not buy. That is the downside. The upside is that many more people will buy because I am making it easier for them and showing trust in them. Put bad experiences in the bin. 95% of people are good.

Don't let the exception become the rule. Don't treat everyone as dishonest just because some are.

Sometimes the need to reciprocate makes life difficult for us for example when a prospect has dealt with another supplier over some years they may feel a loyalty to the existing supplier in return for the years of perceived good service. Prospects will tend to go back to their existing supplier with your quote and use it as a negotiation tool rather than give you the business. We will deal with this in the section on Negotiation.

For reciprocation to work successfully for you it is essential to give with no expectation that you will get something back!

People don't like to be proved wrong

It is amazing the lengths people will go to prove they aren't wrong! They will spend time and energy convincing you and end up conceding that whilst they are not wrong they weren't completely right!

In any event the best strategy in selling certainly isn't trying to prove prospects are wrong!

Scarcity

British Airways decided that economically they could no longer operate a Concorde flight. Immediately after the announcement the bookings increased. The service hadn't improved nor had the prices dropped, the only reason for the increase seemed to be that people were attracted by scarcity.

If you want to sell a car or house the easiest way is to invite potential buyers to view at exactly the same time! It would appear that the thought that someone else may get it is enough to cause people to buy.

The problem with scarcity is people advertise abundance, huge stocks, 24 hour opening, instant credit etc. The clever thing is to do this without abusing scarcity.

In particular use scarcity to help people make decisions. Why would a prospect say 'yes' today if there are no benefits or consequences of putting off the decision until tomorrow? We need to be mindful of using, genuine, scarcity rather than being harmed by abundance.

Liking

I am not a huge fan of this mainly because salespeople get the wrong message. Experiments support the view that we buy from people we like. We may do but more importantly we buy from people we trust.

I have heard salespeople say the first thing you need to do is sell yourself. Some salespeople clearly shouldn't sell themselves because the product isn't very good!

Liking is an important aspect in building trust and we will look at this in greater detail in the Relationship Selling section.

Comparison Theory

Comparison Theory states that we never judge things in isolation we compare everything.

For example try this experiment.

Fill three buckets with water, one with hot water, one with really cold water and one with water at room temperature.

Put one of your hands in the hot water and at the same time put your other hand in the cold water. Keep them there for a few minutes.

Take both hands out and at then immediately plunge them both into the room temperature water. You will experience the odd sensation that one hand feels that the water is quite warm whilst the other feels that the water is very cold. That is comparison theory at work.

Another experiment you could try is asking people to judge the weight of an object. Say you take three objects, one weighing 1 kilo, the second weighing 2 kilos and a third weighing 3 kilos.

Give some people the 3 kilo weight, without telling them the weight. Ask them to hold for it one minute and then give them the 2 kilo weight and ask them to guess how much it weighs.

Do the same with another group and this time give them the one kilo weight to hold for one minute then the 2 kilo weight to guess what the weight is. You will find on average the people who hold the heavy weight first will consistently estimate the 2 kilo weight as lighter than the group who hold the 1 kilo weight first.

What does this mean for selling? Three things:

1.) You rarely sell a shirt after you sell a tie but often sell a tie to go with a shirt. Remember the value to selling add-ons.

2.) Use 'Top Down Selling' as described earlier.

3.) Never mention a price without first mentioning a higher price. The higher price must always be in the same region as the actual price otherwise this technique can work against you.

Some examples of the use of Comparison Theory:

Someone telephones you to ask the current price of your fastest selling product. You could answer 'I think it is £60 let me check ..... no it is actually £57 now'. Note that it has to be in the region or this can actually work against you. If you said 'I think it is £352 ..... no it is actually £24' it would work against you. This is because you are obviously using a technique.

Many direct salespeople selling double glazing, kitchens and conservatories have used a technique called 'Price Conditioning', which uses Comparison Theory. I have included this merely as an explanation of Comparison Theory rather than advocating its use.

To explain price conditioning let me take an example of someone selling a kitchen. They turn up for the appointment at the prospects home. After some warm up conversation they ask the prospects thoughts about a kitchen.

They ask them if they have a budget – guessing the prospect will say 'No'. After having a quick look at their kitchen the 'designer', being very experienced, knows that for the solid wooden kitchen the prospect mentioned earlier they are probably looking at £8,000.

Then the salesperson price conditions them to £10,000. It is done by mentioning the sum £10,000 as many times as possible in the presentation. Innocently of course never connecting directly the £10,000 as the cost of their kitchen.

Some of the things they may say are:

'The average cost of a wooden kitchen is £10,000'

'Look at the quality of these hinges and if you are spending around £10,000 you would expect the hinges to be top quality wouldn't you'

'Have you thought of finance?' Everybody answers they will pay cash to this question. 'Aha so you are the type of person that keeps ten grand under the bed are you? Even if you do have £10,000 under the bed I would like to give you an idea of how our finance package would make it easier for you'. Then they sell the benefits of using their own in-house finance package.

They illustrate the finance costs saying 'I don't know how much your kitchen will cost, but say you were borrowing £10,000 which is an easy figure to use'

All the time their objective is solely to mention £10,000 as often as possible.

When they price up the kitchen at £8,500 mentally the prospect feels they have saved £1500. Then they do a 'drop close' 'If you sign on the night you can get it for £8000'.

You probably wouldn't believe that anyone could be so gullible. It doesn't work every time but I can assure you that it does work.

When giving prices you should also use comparison theory. Always compare usual price, retail price, normal price, alternative product price or some other price so that the final price seems to be lower.

You can use other products as well for example saying the Kodak is £500 and the Xerox is only £471

Comparison theory can also be used with a time objection. The prospect wants it now and you don't have it in stock and it will take three weeks to get it. Compare the three weeks with how long they will keep the product. If they keep a product for 10 years it is worth waiting rather than buying a product that isn't exactly what they want? Another few weeks won't hurt will it?

Outlook

Some people are pessimists some are optimists although It may not be as black and white as that.

Sometimes I am optimistic and sometimes pessimistic. It depends on the product I am buying. For example when I bought a new computer, I was pessimistic. I am worried about it breaking down and the technical support and warranties seem important. When buying a vacuum cleaner I certainly was optimistic and didn't care about guarantees.

I guess this comes from previous experience with these products. I have never had a vacuum cleaner that broke down. I have always needed technical support on every computer I have bought (and most software programmes too).

Selling to optimists must be different from selling to pessimists. I will deal with this in a later section.

Enthusiasm is infectious. The only thing that transfers quicker is un-enthusiasm! As a salesperson you need to be enthusiastic.

I worked for a company that had fantastic products. We demonstrated how good they were and the demonstrations had a high visual impact. New salespeople would often start with the company and their sales would get off to a flying start. After few months however, their sales would dip. The only explanation was that the salesperson got a little bored with the demonstration. They forgot prospects were seeing it for the first time.

When people ask 'how are you?' the answer should be 'great'. Our usual answer? – 'Not Bad'! Bad? Who talks about bad? Why is the focus on the negative?

When others ask 'How's business?' the answer should always be positive. A recession is a great time to use a positive implied statement. 'Our business has increased, I think the recession has meant that customers have to look for better value for money'!

Need for Praise
We actively seek the approval of others.

If you combine this with our need for consistency you can praise someone when they make a decision. If you praise someone for being very decisive they will find it harder to avoid making a decision later.

If you tell someone that you like them they will find it harder to dislike you. Be sincere. I have found something to like in every prospect. .

Buying Motivators
The three buying motivators (in order of importance) are:

1.) Habit

2.) Emotion

3.) Logic

Habit
If you think of all your spending what percentage do you spend on something you have bought before from someone you regularly buy from?

Supermarkets calculated that it took four visits to a competitor's supermarket to develop a new habit of shopping there. Their answer? They invented loyalty cards.

Loyalty cards were not invented with the intention of giving needless discounts. They were invented to identify buying patterns. The supermarket could identify when you were likely to be buying elsewhere and they could shower you with personalised offers to bring you back. They needed to stop you from developing your habit with a competitor.

Overcoming habit can be very difficult. Get the prospect to examine the habit. Complimenting the existing supplier (reverse psychology), will often achieve positive results in this respect.

Use consistency questions to pre-close e.g. 'what action would you take if we provided you with a more attractive option?' 'how would you feel about leaving your existing supplier?'

Get commitment before providing full details. Use ballpark figures and general details until you are getting commitment. Use reciprocation by explaining how much time, effort and costs are involved in getting final quotations.

Emotion

Of the emotions fear and greed have the biggest impact on our decision to buy. Most marketing strategies try to combine fear with greed e.g. 'special rate offer ends soon!'

Cialdini tells a wonderful story about using greed to sell. Two brothers have a tailoring business. One brother serving a customer is a little deaf. He is always asking the customers to repeat themselves because he is hard of hearing. The customer seems to be interested in a blue suit and has asked the price. The 'deaf' brother shouts to the other one

'Bob, how much is this blue suit?'

The answer comes back '$70' (suits are obviously much cheaper in America!)

'How much did you say - $50?

'$70' (said a little louder).

He turns to the prospect and says 'Bob says the suit is $50'. People have bought the suit and are out of the shop as quickly as possible before the 'deaf' brother discovers his 'mistake'.

So greed is very motivational but avoiding pain is even more motivational.

Regret
Daniel Kahneman conducted a study describing two people who were delayed by half an hour in a traffic jam on the way to the airport. Both were delayed enough that they both missed flights on which they were booked, one of them by half an hour and the second by only five minutes (because their flight had been delayed for 25 minutes). The results showed that the second person would be more upset than the first.

In a second study both were delayed by a traffic jam on the way to the airport. One decided to change route to avoid the jam and the other stuck to their original route. Both missed their flights by only five minutes. In this case the person who changed route experienced more regret than the person who stuck to the original plan.

The same effect happens with suppliers. Prospects would experience more regret if they change suppliers and something undesirable happened. The increased regret would be apparent even if the same thing had happened if they hadn't changed suppliers.

Another fascinating finding was that, everything else being equal, most people are much more interested in making sure they don't lose money than they are in actually making it. When we mentally balance the books, we put more weight on the value of a loss, giving it two to three times the importance we give to the value of the size of gain. This has been confirmed in hundreds of subsequent experiments.

If you ask a prospect 'what do we need to do to get your business?' (Still a bad question)! The most popular answer is 'low price'. Despite this we know that low price is not a motivator to buy. If you ask 'what costs your business money?' no one will ever say your prices. This is because whatever you charge them it doesn't costs them money. They simply pass your prices on to their customers. What will cost their business money are the losses caused by poor service. They cannot charge their customer an extra 2 hours for labour because a delivery from a supplier was late. They cannot get a customer to pay for replacing a poor quality product they used. The focus comes away from price altogether to service and product quality issues.

Change your questioning style from finding out needs to looking for pain. What hurts the company? How do they lose money? When things go wrong what happens and what do they have to do to put it right?

I was working with a distributor recently and we discussed this. To test the theory one of the regional managers went out the very next day and asked his major clients how they lost money. He reckoned he got to understand more about their buying motivation in one meeting than he had in ten years of dealing with the client.

Avoiding pain is much more motivational than going for pleasure.

Logic

If all purchases made were logical then the economies of the world would collapse. Logic is the least likely thing to convince a buyer.

Implied and Explicit statements

How we respond to these is very different.

When we hear explicit claims our natural instinct is to think negatively. When we hear implied statements our natural instincts are to add 2 + 2 together.

I need to sort implied and explicit into three groups.

- Explicit Facts

- Explicit Claims

- Implied Statements

Explicit facts:

'We have 26 branches in the UK and 300 branches throughout the world.'

This may imply things about your organisation, big successful, lots of other people buy from you etc. You may call it a bragging fact because that's how most prospects hear them. They generally don't listen to this type of information unless it is relevant to them.

Explicit facts are used only to support implied statements.

Explicit claims:

'Best pizza in town'

'Biggest stock in the UK'

I have noticed that some companies haven't really got the hang of 'best'!

It is best not to use explicit claims.

Implied statements

These are designed to get listeners or readers to work out a conclusion for themselves. If they do work it out themselves then they will defend their own conclusion.

Let me give an example:

You read in a newspaper that a factory burned down and the owners were in financial trouble. You have probably already concluded that there is a good chance that the factory owners deliberately set the fire **because** they were in financial trouble. It is a natural instinct.

If the fire was a small incident newspapers usually share reports from groups such as Reuters. Another newspaper picks up exactly the same report and prints it, this time placing slightly more emphasis on the financial trouble. Giving details of a previous business that went bankrupt etc.

Then they refer to a previous story about arson.

In six months time you are likely to believe that the business owners burned down their own factory to get compensation and may even have extended that into a life prison sentence!

Previously I used a photograph of cashmere clothing that I took in an airport. You probably thought that 120% cashmere is impossible. Look again, the labelling in the photograph is 100% correct! That is the power of implied statements. If you want to argue that I am wrong then again that is the power of implied statements. You have made a connection and now you want to defend your belief.

A company called 120% Cashmere Ltd makes the garments! There is a little sign in the bottom right stating the garment is €118 and is 100% Pure Cashmere.

Some phrases that imply things are:

- We definitely know how much it can cost you if you don't get a delivery in time, which is why we have ten vehicles operating from our depot. This is using an implied statement followed by an explicit fact.

- The traditional approach is .....
  Use the approach you believe your competitor will recommend! This implies that you have a newer, more effective approach.

- Their cheapest solution is .....
  Cheap implies all sorts of things as well as cost. When discussing your own solutions talk about 'our least expensive solution' or 'our highest value solution'.

Words that imply things:

- Recent study

- Cheap

- Conventional

- Traditional

- Modern

- Popular

You should never refer to any of your products as cheap or cheaper. It is OK to refer to competitor's products as cheaper. Cheap implies poor quality rather than low price.

If your prices are higher and you are successful it implies the people who are buying from you know something others don't. Never be frightened by someone telling you a competitor is cheaper. If a prospect tells me that someone is cheaper I simply acknowledge that. We know there are cheaper products available in the market place.

Of course you need a different strategy if you believe you are selling exactly the same product as your competitors. In this case you may also use implied statements to move prospects from the similar product to your exclusive range. For example 'We used to sell a lot more of them but now we sell more of these'.

Labels and Filters

We filter information through the labels we create.

I run this exercise with retail sales people: I divide the delegates into 2 groups

- Group A I ask to go outside the room

- Group B are asked to remain

I brief both groups separately. Group A is asked to think of names that salespeople, sometimes, use to describe customers? I have run this exercise many times and believe me I have heard everything including some that can't be mentioned in a book!

Group B are asked to think of words that would express how customers would like to be thought of by the salespeople when they enter a shop.

Group A examples:

- Time Wasters

- Be Backs – say they will be back (sometimes called Arnies!)

- Know-alls

- Skinflints

- Something for Nothings

- Nerds

- Brochure Hunters

- Tyre kickers

- Chatterboxes

Group B examples:

- Important

- Knowledgeable

- Serious buyer

- Friendly

- Streetwise (not gullible)

- Affluent

Quite a disconnect isn't there. I then ask if salespeople feel they can keep the nasty words in their head they (sometimes) think and treat people, as they would like to be treated? Almost everyone thinks they can but the evidence is against them.

Have you ever been treated as if you were a time waster? How did the salesperson convey that message? No one would say you were wasting their time but somehow they conveyed what they were thinking by what I describe as non-verbal leakage!

The expression 'time waster' staggers me. Someone gets out of bed, dresses, jumps in their car, finds a parking space and comes into your shop simply to waste your time. Any salesperson that thinks these warm leads are time wasters needs a spell of cold calling to appreciate their opportunity.

A study by a bathroom manufacture looked at buying behaviour of prospects.

How many showrooms or DIY stores would the average person visit before making a purchase? Course delegates usually think about three. The correct answer was fourteen!

How long would the process take from entering the first showroom to the purchase? Course delegates usually say about three months. The correct answer is two years. I have recently bought two bathrooms and for the first eighteen months I didn't even realise that I needed a bathroom. My wife was looking in bathroom showrooms locally, when with friends nationally, even when on holiday internationally.

Selling is a little like playing in a golf tournament. You can't win the tournament at any hole but you can lose it at every hole. You can't make a sale every time you meet a prospect but you can lose a prospect every time you meet them. Thinking about prospects as time wasters probably loses all the people who are in the information gathering stage.

So generally we give people labels, they can be nice labels but I suspect most are not.

I am always surprised of the proportions – dozens of negative or rude names for every nice name. Not a great starting point for selling.

I then pick a delegate to help me explain filters. I ask the groups to split again. To one group I say the delegate is my best friend and I have recommended them for a promotion. To the other group I tell them we both went for a promotion and I didn't get it, we were rivals.

When the groups get back together again I walk up to the delegate and say:

'I hear you have just been promoted. Well done. I don't have time right now, but how about I give you a call and we can have a drink together to celebrate'

Now the question is what do the groups think about the interaction and me?

Group A think I was being sincere and will call to organise a celebration.

Group B think I was insincere, I won't call and I am bitter.

Everyone heard the same words, they heard the same intonation and they saw the same body language. These are the classic verbal and non-verbal clues used by body language specialists. So what was different?

The only things that differed were the labels they had. One group had the label 'friend' whilst the other group had the label 'rival'. So not only do we give people labels we filter any information we receive through these labels.

If we label people as time wasters we filter their actions through that label and confirmation bias says we prove that we are right!

Choice

We can find it difficult to make choices. Most of us can decide between two things. It becomes a bit more challenging to decide between three things. More than three and we have all sorts of problems. A friend calls it 'paralysis by choice'

I remember working with a car manufacturer. Imagine someone going into a dealer and asking for a colour (say a green car) that wasn't in the range. The sales person tells their manager they could have had a sale of a green car.

The prospect would go to another dealer and then another, always looking for a green car. There is only one prospect and now three or four requests for a green car. Sales managers passed this information back to manufacturers who would conclude they were losing sales for the lack of green coloured cars

With the ease of contacting numerous people on the internet today, in the same situation, you could now have 50 requests for a green car. That is 50 sales managers asking manufacturers for green cars. The manufacturer now thinks there is a demand for green cars and starts making them.

This is a true story and when the manufacturer started painting cars in proportion to the requests they found little demand for certain colours.

The proliferation of your product range comes from a story that is rooted in this process. I was working in Romania and a purchasing manager said: 'Why is it we have 100,000 product lines and my salespeople want 100,001? Why do they want to sell something they don't have rather than something they do?'

Increase the number of choices you give and your sales will drop. Many times I have started shopping for something and given up because the decision was becoming too complex. Have a look on the Nespresso website. I couldn't cope with the choice despite their product comparison system and so I took the easiest choice – I asked a friend which one they bought!

Have you thought about how many different types of jeans you can buy today?

Forget colours for a moment:

Regular   Easy fit   Slim fit

Relaxed fit   Baggy   Extra baggy

Cowboy   Straight leg   Bootleg

Button fly   Nylon Zip   Metal Zip

Stonewashed   Acid washed   Skinny leg

Distressed or just a little bit sad

Have I missed some?

How can anyone possibly make a choice when faced with these numbers? Uncertainty is a sure-fire way to get people to do nothing. Tell people there may be an update, or a new product coming soon and see what happens to your sales.

The role of a salesperson is to avoid objections and that includes choices. You have to make it easy for people to make the 'right' choice.

THE SIX MOST IMPORTANT WORDS IN SELLING

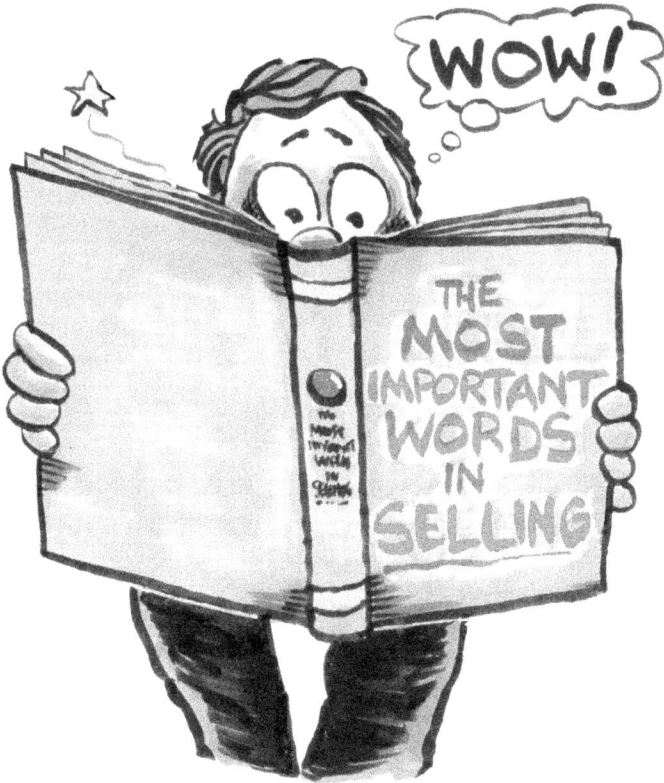

Are single words important? You bet they are. What if we changed the name of the defence industry to the attack industry or the killing industry? A homebuilder changed their sales dramatically by changing the name of an area from Docklands to Harbourside. What if your street was changed from Slag Hill to Paradise Row?

Some words in English seem to have more power than others, because of what they imply, and I have identified six of them here:

Why
Our history with the word is such that it is implied that we are wrong! When you were a child your parents would almost exclusively ask 'Why?' in negative situations. 'Why did you jump in the puddle?' 'Why did you fail the exam?' 'Why did you hit your sister?' Almost never would they say 'why were you nice to your brother?' 'Why did you pass the exam?' In these situations they ask 'Why?' but using different words. 'What do you think helped you to pass the exam?'

Because of this 'Why?' can be a very dangerous and very powerful word.

'Why?' can be perceived as a very aggressive word. It challenges the responder to come up with a justification. Never start a sentence with 'Why?', always disguise the word in the sentence. For example 'that is very interesting would you mind if I ask you why that is?' Another way is to avoid the word altogether, 'how come' asks the same thing but isn't as aggressive.

Never ask 'Why?' in any negative situation. You will only make it harder for yourself.

Some examples of negative things that may be said

'I don't buy xxx from you'

'I don't like your xxxx'

'I prefer to buy those from your competitor'

Any objection

Imagine you ask 'Why?' in any of these situations. All that can possibly happen is that the prospect will defend their statement. Now you would need to prove them to be wrong and people don't like admitting they are wr.. wro.. – not right!

When you ask 'Why?' you lost a piece of business you are getting the logical reasons not the emotional reasons. The emotional reasons are harder to articulate.

Because of this never ask a prospect why you didn't get the business. I know this is controversial so let me state my reasoning:

- The prospect finds it very difficult to articulate the real reasons so they are likely to lead you in the wrong direction.

- They often blame price but Paco Underhill (in 'Why We Buy') found that it was an excuse since over 50% had actually paid more.

- Even if your price is lower prospects normally use lower prices as a negotiation tool with their preferred supplier.

- Even if you are given a real reason, in my experience companies don't and shouldn't change their business to suit a prospect that didn't buy. You should listen to the people that do buy not the people who don't.

If you insist that it gives you information you can rely on, get someone senior to everyone involved in the pitch, to speak to the prospect. There is a chance that a prospect would say to a manager that you underperformed, they don't trust you, you turned up late etc. The politeness principle says they won't tell you.

You should always ask 'why?' when anything positive is said. Ironically we seem to be pre programmed not to ask why in these situations.

For example someone says 'I would prefer to deal with you'. Asking them 'why?' causes them to justify the remark. Because you want to disguise the word in the sentence you may ask 'that is really interesting, would you mind if I asked you why that is?' They will now tell you many reasons why they prefer to deal with you. This has the impact of making it harder for them to negotiate on price.

Asking the question 'why?' at the right time will help prevent buyer's remorse (when purchasers start wondering if they have made the right decision). It increases loyalty and avoids price negotiations.

Examples of positive things said

'I buy xxx only from you'

'I prefer your xxxx'

'I prefer to buy those from you'

Any buying signal

A word of caution; 'I need to think about it' has to be treated carefully with regard to asking 'why?' As a salesperson you would like them to think about it. In this circumstance asking 'why?' may produce good results. The difficulty is this statement is sometimes used as a smokescreen for a hidden objection. Asking 'why?' in these circumstances would be counterproductive. I will deal with 'I need to think about it' in the objections chapter.

Because

The word 'because' is the second most powerful word in selling. People like to have a reason for doing things. The word 'because' also implies you are an expert because that is the language that experts tend to use!

Robert Cialdini conducted a great experiment when he asked actors to go to someone sitting on a park bench and asked them to move. The actors had to follow a script giving a reason they wanted the person to move. For example the actor would say 'Would you please move to the middle of the bench, I would like to sit at this end?' Cialdini measured how many people agreed to move over. In the alternative script the word 'because' was added, 'would you please move to the middle of the bench **because** I would like to sit at this end? Nothing else was changed; the message was exactly the same. When the word 'because' was added four times more people agreed to move. Cialdini concluded that people like to have a reason for doing something. He repeated the experiment with people waiting to use a photocopier and achieved the same results.

There are two situations when using the word 'because' will improve your results:

When you are asking someone to do something.
Any time you ask someone to do something always use the word because in the sentence because they are more likely to do it.

Examples:

> 'Can we arrange a meeting for next week because I would like to find out more about your needs?'

> 'Can you sign here because then I can check the stock is available?'

> 'You need to pay a deposit of 20% because we have to hold the stock for you'

When giving your opinion
Anytime you are giving your opinion you should use the word because in the sentence because then you are giving your professional expertise rather than your opinion.

> 'I think this one is better for you because .....'

> 'I don't think we could do that because .....'

'I think this is a better quality product because .....'

But (or rather And)

The word 'but' does something in our head that we seem to have little control over. When we hear the word 'but' we immediately seem to process this as an argument. It encourages the listener stop listening and think of counter arguments. It implies an argument even though there are two uses of the word. Firstly there is 'but', secondly there is 'and also'.

I have seen people in violent agreement! They think they are arguing because both keep using 'but' and they are making the same point. They are actually saying the same thing and agreeing with each other.

In experiments it becomes clear that we almost stop listening after the word 'but'. We are, at best, only listening sufficiently to get information to counter the speaker's argument.

You can probably recognise when people say 'you are right but .....' they mean you are not right!

There are acceptable uses of the word 'but'. For example when you are saying you, as opposed to others are wrong e.g. 'I thought I was right but now I know I am wrong'.

The simple rule is if you can easily substitute the word 'and' then use it instead.

We will explore this more in the Objections chapter.

Try and Definitely

'Try' implies they possibility or even probability of failure. Definitely implies certainty. I will deal with these two words together.

Everybody tries. When last did you hear a salesperson saying they know their service is substandard? Everyone claims that they 'try' to give good service. They 'try' to provide good after-sales service. They 'try to respond promptly'. The problem is that everyone is trying!

So using the word 'try' will never differentiate. It can't differentiate. To do so you must use 'definitely'. The problem is you are under enormous pressure not to commit because you know that things do go wrong.

There is a way to use definitely that doesn't commit and it's extremely powerful.

'We definitely understand how important it is for our customers to have deliveries within two hours, which is why we operate with four delivery vehicles from this branch'. Because this implies you deliver within two hours people naturally think positively and will agree that your delivery service is good (if, on balance, it is of course!).

'We definitely know how infuriating it is when a product fails'

'We definitely appreciate the trouble that poor service causes'

'We definitely recognise how much poor service can cost a customer'

Please don't say 'We definitely try to .....'!

Risk
Risk implies a lack of logic. Why take a risk if you don't have to? In general people would prefer to avoid taking risks.

The only time people will actually prefer to take risks is when they are guaranteed to lose if they don't take a risk. So rich people wouldn't take the risk of robbing a bank to increase their wealth but the same people seem to be prepared to cheat the tax authorities to avoid a guaranteed loss of paying income tax. The decision-making is different even though the consequences (going to jail) may be the same.

It is possible to get prospects to take a risk by presenting a solution as a guaranteed loss. For example I was working with Private Bankers, they can present a recommended investments as more risky but the alternative is to lose value compared with inflation. Investments that are tax-efficient are generally more speculative for this reason.

Where 'risky' is more useful is to help with decision-making. To help people make the right choice present alternatives as being slightly more risky.

A good phrase for salespeople to use is 'This is our solution and if you have to take a risk with a cheaper product then I would certainly understand that'.

So these are general aspects of behaviour from both prospects and us that we need to be careful of when selling. Let's consider some of the specific behaviours of prospects so that we can treat people as individuals.

'MOTIVATIONAL' FACTORS AFFECTING BUYERS

DEAL WITH THE BEHAVIOUR

'I cannot go fishing and use what I like as bait - the bait must appeal to the fish'

Dale Carnegie

I work on behaviours rather than personality although on most courses people seem to confuse the two. The small problems this may cause are easily outweighed by the benefits of dealing differently with the four types.

I categorise behaviour based on the following model:

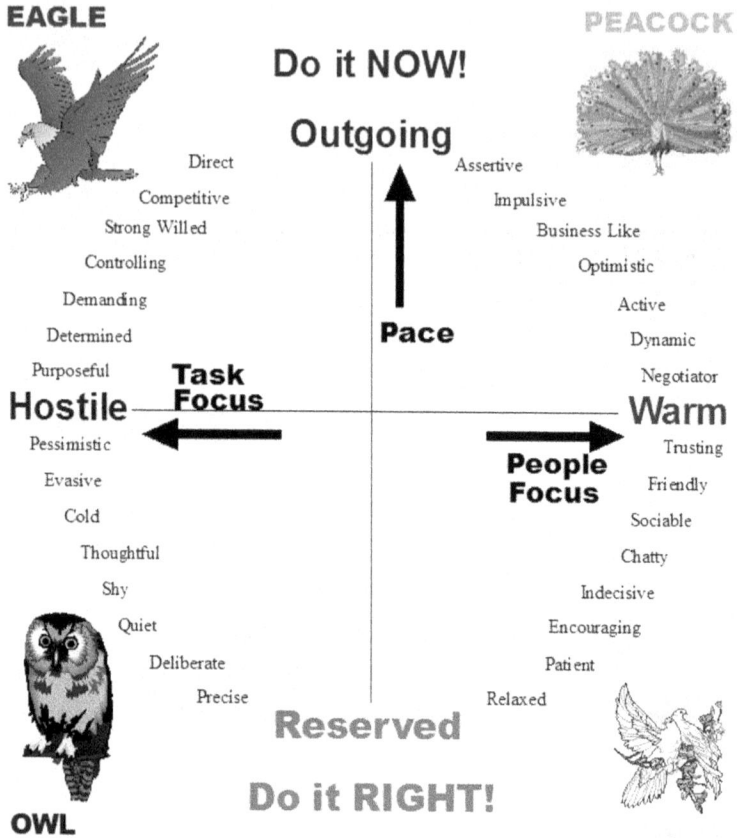

EAGLE

PEACOCK

Do it NOW!

Outgoing

Direct

Assertive

Competitive

Impulsive

Strong Willed

Business Like

Controlling

Optimistic

Demanding

Active

Determined

Pace

Dynamic

Purposeful

Task Focus

Negotiator

Hostile

Warm

Pessimistic

Trusting

Evasive

People Focus

Friendly

Cold

Sociable

Thoughtful

Chatty

Shy

Indecisive

Quiet

Encouraging

Deliberate

Patient

Precise

Relaxed

Reserved

Do it RIGHT!

OWL

The model uses two factors to classify behaviours.

- How important is time to the person – do they need to get results quickly?

- How friendly are they. Do they want to get involved with the salesperson or is the salesperson a necessary evil?

A question I am regularly asked on courses is how do you spot the four different types?

I don't actually analyse people as I meet with them, I don't even think of the strategy for dealing with each behaviour type during a meeting. When I am selling I deal with people in my normal way, most of us do.

The only time that I think of the behaviour model is when things are not going as well as I would like. When this happens I keep a central thought in my head to get the meeting back on track. I will share with you the signals I use and my central thoughts for each of the four types.

I base the behaviours on a model, which is similar to Jung's Personality trait model however it is not useful as a personality model for several reasons:

- It would take a long time to assess a prospect's or a prospect's personality.

- Most psychologists agree you cannot change someone's personality but you can change their behaviour very easily.

- You must deal with the situation and the behaviour! If a 'Dove' has a complaint there is no sense in asking 'Did you see the football last night?' It is the easiest way to change behaviour although it may be from 'Dove' to 'Eagle'!

- We can all behave in each of the four styles. For example I am an 'Eagle' when I buy a house (I don't generally trust Estate Agents), I am an 'Owl' when the taxman calls (and I would advise you to be as well!). I am a 'Dove' when I get a haircut (I have plenty of time and it pays to be friendly) and I am a 'Peacock' when buying a holiday.

It is easy to judge someone's behaviour and research has shown that most people make the judgements on which this behaviour model is based within the first seven seconds.

All you need to decide is whether the prospect is in a hurry for a result, in this case they are above the line. Dominant people push things along and don't like taking more time than necessary.

Secondly are they friendly? If they are friendly their behaviour is to the right of the line and so:

- **Time Important and Friendly**   'Peacock'

- **Time Important and Not Friendly**   'Eagle'

- **Time Not Important and Not Friendly** 'Owl'

- **Time Not Important and Friendly**   'Dove'

The reason I use birds to describe the types is because the characteristics of the birds give an indication of the behaviour to expect:

The 'Eagle' is a predator, they will use attack as the best form of defence.

'Owls' are wise, they will sit quietly and gather information before making a move.

'Doves' are lovey 'dovey! As long as there is no conflict they are happy.

'Peacocks' like to display what they know, they are streetwise and like everyone to see them strutting about.

Explanation of the four Behaviour Types -

'Eagle'

They want action and they want it now! They like to control the situation and can easily become aggressive if they feel they are not being dealt with well.

They are likely to want to be attended to quickly and will sometimes complain loudly in a packed showroom about the lack of attention. They have no fear about others hearing them and hearing their complaint or moan.

They also often use sweeping generalisations – 'You people are all the same and can't be trusted'.

Typical 'Eagle' behaviour approaches are:

'How much discount will you give me on that?' (The first words they utter!)

'Don't use any of you sales spiel on me!'

'Owl'

'Owl' behaviour typically indicates that they feel the best form of defence is to play their cards close to their chest. They will often enter a showroom with the intention of avoiding salespeople altogether. You try to engage them in conversation and find it is very difficult. They often ask for brochures or more information and may even have a bag full of brochures from other potential suppliers as well (although they are more likely to leave these in their car to avoid you seeing them). The best sign you are dealing with an 'Owl' is you find that you are doing most of the talking!

They are also experts in getting you to answer your own questions! For example you ask the 'Owl' 'What type of investments are you thinking about?' They may say something like 'I am not sure what options are available?' and you find yourself taking them through the entire range of possibilities.

Typically an 'Owl' will not approach you at all until they are desperate. If you do approach them they may respond by saying 'Do you have any brochures on this?' 'Owls' (and 'Doves') often end by saying they need to think about it.

'Dove'

Someone behaving as a 'Dove' will use friendliness to get what they want. They like to develop relationships with people they buy from and they will generally be chatty. They may beat about the bush and often go off at a tangent.

Because making a decision is not a typical characteristic they may give indications that they have been considering a purchase for some time. For example they may also have some ideas about what they want and say they can't make up their mind between two or three choices.

They may also ask a question that you suspect is a clarification from the last supplier they have been to e.g. 'what is the difference between a low-level cistern and a close coupled one?' or 'what is the difference between a pension and an annuity?'

'Peacock'

The 'Peacock' uses friendly banter and barter to get what they want. They may use your name even though you are not sure how they got it. They will definitely ask for a discount and may do so by offering something in return e.g. 'if I bought two of these from you how much discount would you give me?'

They are most likely to leave the discounting barter to a later stage in the purchase than an 'Eagle'.

They are decisive and usually <u>think</u> they know what they want. They may also offer friendly advice as to how you could increase your efficiency and sales! They can also appear to be knowledgeable about every subject under the sun!

We now need to decide how these people want to be dealt with and so I have devised the following exercise:

For each behaviour type answer the questions as if the prospect is behaving as the 'Eagle', 'Owl', 'Dove' or 'Peacock'.

If the prospect is behaving as an: 'Eagle'

Questioning

- Would you focus on asking questions about the prospect's **Opinions** e.g. 'how do you think the market will react?' or would you concentrate more on questions about **Facts** e.g. 'how many xxxx do you have?' All questions need to be relevant!

- Would you ask more questions about the future or the past?

- Would your focus change at any stage? (Assume that their behaviour doesn't change). You will need some facts and therefore will need to ask factual questions with everyone but which would you focus on.

Would you use 'small talk' to warm up these prospects?

Interrupting
Would you interrupt this prospect?

What would you do if they were wrong? Would you tell them they are wrong?

Short Gaps in the Conversation
Should you encourage this or jump in whenever you have the chance?

Your Opinion
Should you give your opinion? What would you do if they asked for it?

Loyalty and Price Sensitivity
Should you treat them as if they are loyal and/or price sensitive? The Options are:

Loyal and Not Price Sensitive	Not Loyal and Not Price Sensitive
Loyal and Price Sensitive	Not Loyal and Price Sensitive

Detail or Overview?

Do these people want detailed explanations or an overview?

Should you prepare an agenda for a meeting, if so why? (Not Retail Selling)

How do these people react when things go wrong?

What added value is a good salesperson for this prospect?

For example a bad salesperson is no added value, what does a good salesperson do that is appreciated by this person?

If the prospect is behaving as an: 'Owl'

Questioning
- Would you focus on asking questions about the prospect's **Opinions** e.g. 'how do you think the market will react?' or would you concentrate more on questions about **Facts** e.g. 'how many xxxx do you have?' All questions need to be relevant!

- Would you ask more questions about the future or the past?

- Would your focus change at any stage? (Assume that their behaviour doesn't change). You will need some facts and therefore will need to ask factual questions with everyone but which would you focus on.

Would you use 'small talk' to warm up these prospects?

Interrupting
Would you interrupt this prospect?

What would you do if they were wrong? Would you tell them they are wrong?

Short Gaps in the Conversation
Should you encourage this or jump in whenever you have the chance?

Your Opinion
Should you give your opinion? What would you do if they asked for it?

Loyalty and Price Sensitivity
Should you treat them as if they are loyal and/or price sensitive? The Options are:

Loyal and Not Price Sensitive   Not Loyal and Not Price Sensitive

Loyal and Price Sensitive   Not Loyal and Price Sensitive

Detail or Overview?

Do these people want detailed explanations or an overview?

Should you prepare an agenda for a meeting, if so why? (Not Retail Selling)

How do these people react when things go wrong?

What added value is a good salesperson for this prospect?

For example a bad salesperson is no added value, what does a good salesperson do that is appreciated by this person?

If the prospect is behaving as an: 'Dove'

Questioning

- Would you focus on asking questions about the prospect's **Opinions** e.g. 'how do you think the market will react?' or would you concentrate more on questions about **Facts** e.g. 'how many xxxx do you have?' All questions need to be relevant!

- Would you ask more questions about the future or the past?

- Would your focus change at any stage? (Assume that their behaviour doesn't change). You will need some facts and therefore will need to ask factual questions with everyone but which would you focus on.

Would you use 'small talk' to warm up these prospects?

Interrupting
Would you interrupt this prospect?

What would you do if they were wrong? Would you tell them they are wrong?

Short Gaps in the Conversation
Should you encourage this or jump in whenever you have the chance?

Your Opinion
Should you give your opinion? What would you do if they asked for it?

Loyalty and Price Sensitivity

Should you treat them as if they are loyal and/or price sensitive? The Options are:

Loyal and Not Price Sensitive	**Not Loyal and Not Price Sensitive**
Loyal and Price Sensitive	**Not Loyal and Price Sensitive**

Detail or Overview?

Do these people want detailed explanations or an overview?

Should you prepare an agenda for a meeting, if so why? (Not Retail Selling)

How do these people react when things go wrong?

What added value is a good salesperson for this prospect?

For example a bad salesperson is no added value, what does a good salesperson do that is appreciated by this person?

If the prospect is behaving as an: 'Peacock'

Questioning

- Would you focus on asking questions about the prospect's **Opinions** e.g. 'how do you think the market will react?' or would you concentrate more on questions about **Facts** e.g. 'how many xxxx do you have?' All questions need to be relevant!

- Would you ask more questions about the future or the past?

- Would your focus change at any stage? (Assume that their behaviour doesn't change). You will need some facts and therefore will need to ask factual questions with everyone but which would you focus on.

Would you use 'small talk' to warm up these prospects?

Interrupting

Would you interrupt this prospect?

What would you do if they were wrong? Would you tell them they are wrong?

Short Gaps in the Conversation

Should you encourage this or jump in whenever you have the chance?

Your Opinion

Should you give your opinion? What would you do if they asked for it?

Loyalty and Price Sensitivity

Should you treat them as if they are loyal and/or price sensitive? The Options are:

Loyal and Not Price Sensitive	Not Loyal and Not Price Sensitive
Loyal and Price Sensitive	Not Loyal and Price Sensitive

Detail or Overview?

Do these people want detailed explanations or an overview?

Should you prepare an agenda for a meeting, if so why? (Not Retail Selling)

How do these people react when things go wrong?

What added value is a good salesperson for this prospect?

For example a bad salesperson is no added value, what does a good salesperson do that is appreciated by this person?

Dealing with the four types of behaviours:

'Eagle'

Advice if the prospect is behaving as an 'Eagle'
Questioning

You should focus on asking questions about the **future** and avoid, as far as possible, questions about the present and past. Remember every salesperson will ask the 'Eagle' factual questions. Interesting recent studies have shown that 'Eagles' are not that keen on questions such as 'tell me about your business?'

It is amazing how many delegates on courses answer this exercise with **Future** & **Fact** questions. It isn't possible to ask a future fact question. All future questions are opinions. 'When do you plan to start?' 'How long is the project expected to last?' etc.

Your focus may start with Opinion questions and at the very end change to ask some Factual summary questions to ensure you have understood.

The 'Eagle' gets bored with factual questions about the past. You get some evidence of this because the 'Eagle' will often pre-prepare a list of requirements. It saves them time going through the answers to the factual questions.

So an easy thought to keep in your head when dealing with an 'Eagle' is to concentrate on asking **FUTURE** questions e.g. 'what challenges do you see in this project?' 'What are the things that suppliers could do that would cost your business money?'

Would you use 'small talk' to warm up these prospects?
No, why warm up a fire?

Interrupting

Interrupting an 'Eagle' is not a great strategy unless you are a product expert, are more senior than they are or you are physically bigger than them!

Never tell them they are wrong! If you feel you must here are some rules:

- Refer to the above – they are never wrong!

- Get some evidence, preferably in writing, to back up what you want to say

- Give them some way to save face e.g. 'I may have misled you' or 'someone has given you the wrong information' etc.

Short Gaps in the Conversation

This question is the same question as the last one. It is interrupting asked in a different way. In other words if you do not leave short gaps then you are interrupting. Leave a short (less than one second) gap after the 'Eagle' speaks.

Your Opinion

When an 'Eagle' wants your opinion they will give you it! They are not interested in your opinions. Avoid words such as 'think', 'try' or 'hopefully' with them. They don't want to know what you think, they want facts.

Sometimes they ask for your opinion and they only want your opinion if it is the same as theirs. Giving your opinion is risky. Sometimes they have only asked you to trap you! Two Strategies if they ask for your opinion are:

- Leave a short gap to encourage them to speak; they will most probably give you their opinion.

• If that doesn't work ask them a **FUTURE** question.

Loyalty and Price Sensitivity

'Eagles' need to be <u>treated</u> as if they are 'Not Loyal and Price Sensitive'. Make sure everything you propose has a valid and logical reason behind it. There is no point trying to leverage loyalty. Justify all price differences with logical benefits.

These people are slightly more price sensitive so don't play games when pricing, give them the price and stick to it. They don't like people to back down.

Detail or Overview?

You must always stick to overview but when the 'Eagle' asks for detail they expect you to know it. If you don't the worst thing you can do is to bluff your way through. 'I'll find out for you' is a great response only if you do find out - don't forget!

When I am in a situation where I behave as an 'Eagle' the worst thing that anyone can do is to read a brochure or packaging to me. I can read! If you need to read something give the 'Eagle' a brochure at the same time so they can read as well.

Should you prepare an agenda for a meeting, if so why?

Always prepare an agenda for every meeting – you have no idea what the prospects behaviour will be when you arrive. Their personality may be 'Dove' and if they are acting as an 'Eagle' then the agenda may help you.

If the prospect wants to hijack the meeting the agenda can be useful. For example you can say 'that isn't on the agenda for this meeting is it ok if I put it down as an item for our next meeting?'

There is a strong correlation between the number of meetings you have with prospects and your success so always look for opportunities for another meeting. In particular the last item on your agenda could be 'Date of next meeting'.

If a prospect asks about one of your products it would be a great time to get another meeting. Explain that you don't have any literature about the product and that you would like to include that in the next meeting. A good time to test how serious the person is about the need for the product by asking them how quickly they need the information.

How do these people react when things go wrong?
The 'Eagle' is likely to go ballistic! Their bark is worse than their bite. Don't take things personally, Stay calm, distance yourself a little physically and use silence to make sure you never interrupt at this time. Ask future questions.

As an example people often behave as 'Eagle's in a complaint situation. A good way of dealing with this is to ask a 'future' question such as 'I'd like to sort this out for you, what would you like me to do to sort it?'

What added value is a good salesperson for this prospect?
Because time is very important anything you can do to save the 'Eagle' time will be seen as valuable.

On course I often get responses such as be professional, knowledgeable etc. In short these save the prospect time.

The signal that identifies someone behaving as an 'Eagle':
The signal I get with an 'Eagle' is that they are controlling me. They are asking me questions that cause me to be working on what they want to talk about when they want to talk about it. For example the 'Eagle' may ask about discounts or lowest prices when I want to be looking at needs and product differentiation.

In fact 'Eagles' often start buying conversations by discussing prices. I want to start selling conversations with needs and wants.

If I get this signal my entire focus shifts to asking 'future' questions. It is much better asking about their concerns and potential issues than it is asking about their history.

'Owl'
Advice if the prospect is behaving as an 'Owl'

Questioning

The 'Owl' wants to collect information rather than give information. They have a favourite tactic, which is to get you answering your own questions. The only way to stop this is to ask easy questions that only they know the answer to.

These are **Past Factual** questions. Ask them about historical things.

At the end you need to move the 'Owl' towards opinion questions. The objective in selling is to discover the values, beliefs and opinions of the prospect. 'Owls' don't go there quickly. A great implied statement question is 'What were you looking for when you chose your current supplier, advisor etc.?' What is implied, in any answer, is they are not getting what they were looking for.

Would you use 'small talk' to warm up these prospects?

If you are good at it absolutely use small talk. If you are not good at it don't worry. There is no point in doing something that is making you both feel uncomfortable.

Some research suggested that we develop friends through a process of 'progressive self disclosure'. This means when we meet someone we normally start to converse using only factual information. What their name is, where they live, what car they drive etc.

If they respond with similar information we may move on to the next level, opinions. What did they think about the latest news etc.?

The next level would be values, their view of society. We may then move on to beliefs.

At each stage one party may decide that is as deep as they want to go in this friendship. They stop at that level. The other party may continue to disclose at the level below but generally wouldn't move on to a deeper level.

If both parties keep disclosing at a deeper and deeper level you may reach the level at which many females use to describe their best friend. That is someone they could tell their deepest secrets and fears to. Males incidentally are more likely to describe best friends in terms of time spent with them and shared activities.

Instead of asking personal questions of prospects it may be more effective to disclose personal information about yourself first. If that prompts reciprocal disclosure from the prospect you can follow your natural instincts to build rapport. Beware of carrying on with personal disclosure if conversation is stonewalled. I am sure that we have all experienced a complete stranger disclosing unsolicited personal information completely out of the blue.

There are of course rules to this disclosure. It is supposed to be progressive so you can't miss out a level for example by going directly from facts to deep-seated beliefs. Also there are business rules. You wouldn't expect to go to a doctor about your back only for the doctor to say 'Yes my back is even sorer than yours!' Nor would you go to a Bank Manager who discloses that their finances are not in order!

Interrupting

You should never, ever interrupt an 'Owl'. Getting them speaking is hard enough without closing them down.

This is generally understood and answered by most delegates on a course. What may be surprising however is just how often the quieter people are interrupted.

Prepare some strategies for quiet people. Be comfortable with longer periods of silence.

If they are wrong it makes no sense to interrupt them, time isn't critical. Always allow them to save face in the same way as with the 'Eagle'.

Short Gaps in the Conversation

No – have long gaps in the conversation. In particular when your prospect is reading something you need to stop talking. I do this by reading something myself. I find that when I am reading my hearing switches off. Apparently it may be common to most males! Please don't speak while I am reading.

When coaching salespeople I have often picked up that salespeople speak during quieter periods. Often they justify this by claiming that they felt the silence was making the prospect feel uncomfortable. It seems clear to me that the salesperson was uncomfortable with the silence. If the prospect were uncomfortable with the short silence then the prospect would end it by speaking.

Your Opinion

Never answer an 'Owls' request for an opinion with a question. They will see you as being evasive. Having said that they do not want your opinion they are after your professional expertise. To change your opinion into your professional expertise is very simple. You only need to include the word 'because' in the sentence. 'I think this is the best brand because .....'

Loyalty and Price Sensitivity

They are the most loyal and the least price sensitive of the four types. They may been seen as 'shoppers' but when they find someone they can trust – bingo. They won't play games and tend to stick with current relationships.

An easy way to see this is when you are cold calling businesses. The following is a typical (but not good) cold calling approach:

(Salesperson)   I would like to come and see you about our new range of products.

(Prospect)   I am happy with my existing supplier

(S)   Yes I am sure you are but we have a new product that they don't have

(P)   Yes but I don't need any new products

(S)   Can you tell me what other products you are buying from them?

(P)   Sorry, I don't have time to go through this

(S)   But we could save you money on your existing purchases

(P)   I am not interested please don't call again

Now, I know this isn't a good example of selling but it is a typical description of an interaction with an 'Owl'. Irrespective of this prospects personality they do not want to engage in a conversation, they are happy with their existing supplier and they are not interested in saving money. It perfectly describes a person that is 'Loyal and Not Price Sensitive'.

A statistic on prospecting:

83% of people buy within 8 calls!

This works on all sorts of levels. If you call 100 prospects 8 times then 83 of these prospects will meet with you. If you have eight meetings then 83% of the people you meet with will place an order with you. This ignores the quality of the activity, if you are good you can improve dramatically on these figures. This tells me that:

Persistence beats Resistance

On a scarier note 80% of salespeople give up after three contacts. This makes no sense to me.

Look at the following graph. On the left is the number of people who buy and the bottom axis is the number of contacts:

8 Contacts 83% Buy

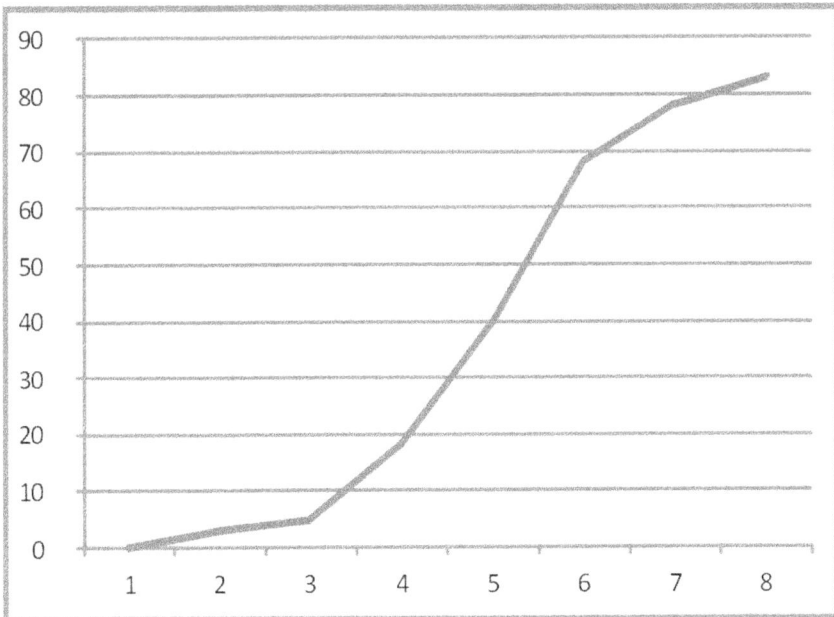

This pattern makes perfect sense to me. How many prospects buy the very first time a salesperson contacts them? Very few in my experience. How about the second contact – perhaps a little more. In a study only five prospects out of 100 had made a purchase within the first three visits. Yet look what happens.

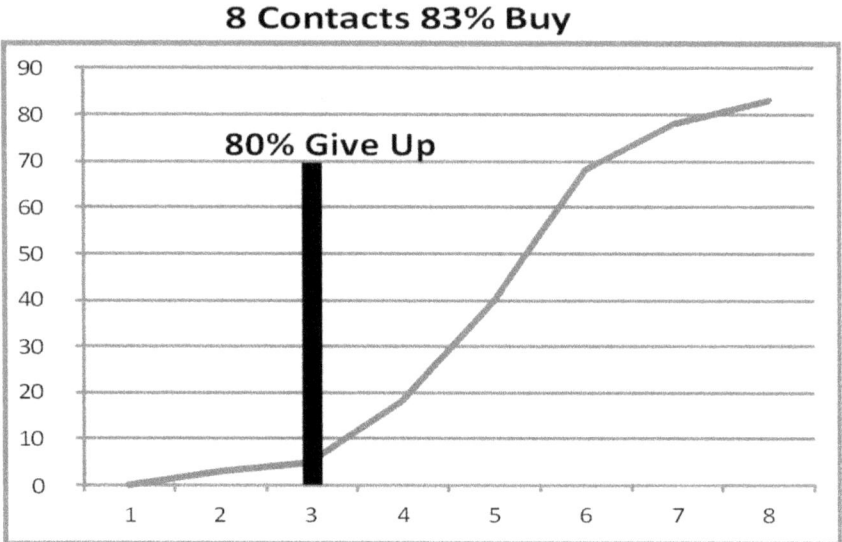

8 Contacts 83% Buy

80% Give Up

(Chart: vertical axis 0–90, horizontal axis 1–8)

What happens is the salespeople have made three calls and had no success so they change the prospects and start again. Their confirmation bias says cold calling is hard and they prove themselves to be correct. Of course what may also happen is that because these approaches are not good the prospect prevents poor salespeople from getting fourth appointments.

Here are some ways to improve your success.

How many prospects do you think are sitting waiting by the phone hoping that a supplier of exactly your products rings them because they can't source them? Exactly! You know that when you call a prospect they will have an existing supplier. Even if they don't get great service how many prospects would say they were too stupid or too lazy to find a good supplier?

A good process then is to think of all the objections a prospect may have and then think about how you may avoid them. Imagine you are going to contact a prospect. Here are some objections you may be faced with:

- 'I don't have time to see you'

- 'I have never heard of you'

- 'I already have a supplier'

- 'We are happy at the moment'

- 'I don't need your product'

You could start by saying:

- You are probably a very busy person and so I .....

- You probably haven't heard of us yet because .....

- You probably already have a supplier that you are happy with and I understand that and the reason for my call is .....

Rules for developing appointments:

- When canvassing an appointment sell the appointment not a product

- Stop selling in the first three contacts. It simply annoys prospects and prevents you getting to the fourth appointment

- Anticipate objections

- Compliment rather than criticise the existing supplier

- Always add value to the prospect in any contact

- If you don't have a reason to call - don't call

- If you have nothing to say, say nothing

- Always look for opportunities for another meeting while you are meeting the prospect

- As far as possible arrange your next meeting at this one. It is easier to cancel a meeting than arrange one

I always get some reaction to the fourth point. It is simply reverse psychology. If you criticise the existing supplier of a prospect you are really saying the prospect is an idiot for buying from them. If you say that their existing supplier is a great company and you know they have a wide range of stock etc. it is amazing how many prospects will contradict you – giving you an opportunity.

Here are some ideas of reasons to contact prospects, which can add value.

New Products:

New products can be a great reason to contact a prospect. When new products are released think about who would benefit from using the product and organise your prospect development calls accordingly. It should be new products to the marketplace rather than new to your company. NB: Never tell an existing customer about a new product until it is actually on the shelf as announcements about new products destroy sales for existing products.

Your Website

Guides and tools on your website that can help prospects to improve efficiency in their business.

Price Rises

'I'm sure your regular supplier has already informed you and I just thought I'd let you know there's going to be a price rise on x product, if you need stock may I suggest you order before the price rise.' You don't need to ask for an order you are informing not selling.

Product Brochures / Technical Guides

Hard to Find Items

Find out the last product they were kept waiting for. Perhaps they have had to keep one of their customers waiting because they couldn't get stock delivered on time. Consider offering to stock a product they use regularly to eliminate future problems for them.

Invite them into your business

You can show them your differentiators and explain how you organise things differently from your competition. Prospects will often visit you when there is no pressure to buy and they are intrigued about your success.

Spare Tyre Approach

Contact a prospect that is trading with someone else and offer to be their 'spare tyre'.

Attend industry or customer nights

They can come to your business and meet some of your prospects. They can gather information about the industry and update their knowledge about changes in regulations or any new initiatives.

The main thing is to add value to the prospect every time you contact them. If you can leave a prospect thinking 'I am glad that salesperson called' then you will get the rewards your hard work deserves.

Detail or Overview?
Very much detail people and be careful. The devil is in the detail. Getting 'Owls' to make a decision is the hardest thing to do and detail makes this harder. Organise the detail to make it simpler. Compare and contrast options and remember to pepper them with the word 'because' to use your professional expertise.

Should you prepare an agenda for a meeting, if so why?
Yes - see the answer for the 'Eagle'.

An agenda will be seen as professional and will probably be followed. Expect the 'Owl' to point out that you have wandered from the agenda!

How do these people react when things go wrong?
They put it down to experience and leave quietly. You may never know what happened.

There is a good lesson in here for lapsed and dormant accounts. These are accounts that have traded in the past and they have stopped trading. Here is how 'normal' salespeople call these people.

(S) 'We are very inefficient, you are probably stupid, please tell me to go away!'

The actual words they say are usually something like this:

(S) 'We have just noticed after six months that you have stopped buying from us. Is there anything you need?'

They seem to think that the prospect is so stupid they can't find another supplier!

People always stop buying from you for a reason. Usually it is a service issue. Do some research with people internally to find out the reason. If you can't find out then assume that you have created the problem and call them on that basis. Something like:

(S) 'We find that when someone leaves us we have usually done something wrong and I have called today because I want to fix that for you. Even if we never do business again I would still like to fix it, what was the issue?'

What added value is a good salesperson for this prospect?
A salesperson is someone for them to place their trust in.

Take your time, show patience and help them through the detail.

The signal that identifies someone behaving as an 'Owl':
The 'Owls' favourite tactic is to get the salesperson to answer their own questions. The signal that you will get with an 'Owl' is that you are doing all the talking. Another signal would be when cold calling they are happy with their existing supplier and don't want to get in to a discussion about it.

If I get this signal I keep a central thought in my head, which is to ask **Past Factual** questions before moving to **Past Opinion** questions.

'Dove'
Advice if the prospect is behaving as a 'Dove'

Questioning
Your success with 'Doves' will not be down to your questioning skills. It really doesn't matter what you ask, past or future, fact or opinion, you will get the information that 'Doves' want to give you rather than answers to your questions.

To see how inefficient 'open' and 'closed' questioning techniques are - test them on a 'Dove'!

The only thing you need to watch for is to judge their future behaviour based on their past behaviour, not on their answers. 'Doves' tend to promise they will buy at some time in the future. They promise they will refer you to their friends. If they haven't done it in the past don't expect that they will do it in the future.

Would you use 'small talk' to warm up these prospects?
Absolutely, there is a strong correlation between time spent with someone and buying. Use it to your advantage. If you do need to cut the small talk short then talk only about their small talk don't add to it! For example if they mention their holiday ask them about it without telling them about yours.

Interrupting
Absolutely, deal with a 'Dove' as you would with any friend. It is OK to interrupt them. An observer would call it interacting with them rather than interrupting them. If you don't interact with them you may be seen as interrogating them.

There is strong evidence that we develop friendships using interrupting. Watch two friends in a bar and you will see them interrupting each other frequently.

If they are wrong interrupt them and always allow them to save face in the same way as with the 'Eagle'.

Short Gaps in the Conversation
There will not be any gaps in the conversation!

Your Opinion
Absolutely, you would give your friend an opinion wouldn't you? You can express it as an opinion as well. 'I think you should .....'

A perfect way to disclose with a 'Dove' is using the phrases 'I shouldn't really be saying this to you but .....' or 'please don't tell my boss I told you this but .....'

Loyalty and Price Sensitivity
This is the tricky one. You need to treat them as 'Not Loyal and Not Price Sensitive'. Close them or lose them! If you leave them to make decisions on their own you risk someone else, who is better than you, taking them out of the market.

This is the hardest thing to deal with for this behaviour. They can combine not objecting with not buying.

Pressure always loses. You will usually lose profit but often you will lose the sale as well. Have you ever genuinely been thinking about a purchase only to walk away because you felt pressured? Did you ever go back? How do you close 'Doves' without putting them under pressure? Be aware that any questions the salesperson asks at this stage will be seen as pressure.

Some prospects say 'I need to think about it' and genuinely do need to think about it. Some prospects use 'I need to think about it' when they have thought about it and decided not to go ahead. We must find a way to distinguish between the two.

The answer lies in our psychological needs explained earlier. We have a need to reciprocate.

Instead of putting someone under pressure do exactly the opposite and watch the reaction. Go out of your way to help them and if they refuse then they have already decided not to buy.

A great example of this is an antiques centre near my home. When my wife looks at something they are eager to let her see it in situ. They will deliver it, leave it for a few days and if she likes it she can pop in and pay for it later. Admittedly it is small value compared with the house! They know where we live; they are delivering it! They know her as a prospect although they haven't always. The point is if you don't trust your prospects you can't expect them to trust you.

Note that if she had already decided she didn't want to buy it she would (and often does) refuse to let them bring it to our home. By offering to be helpful they can easily identify if there is a hidden objection or not.

There is a subtle difference between reciprocity and what the prospect expects of a salesperson. For example the prospect who wants to 'talk to their partner' before making a decision. They would probably expect a salesperson to offer a brochure which would help them discuss it with their partner and so few prospects would refuse a brochure. Accepting a brochure doesn't invoke a need to reciprocate. How about if I offered to go to some trouble such as to take a photograph and email it to them? In this case people with a hidden objection are more likely to refuse to let you go to the trouble of taking a photograph. I could increase the feeling of obligation simply by offering to get a friend (a professional photographer) to take the photograph.

The point of offering something is to identify whether the prospect has a hidden objection or not.

Tailor the offering to your business. For example, a business I worked with had expensive catalogues. They didn't really give them to prospects they were more of a technical publication to help salespeople. When they let a prospect take one home often it wouldn't come back. We solved the problem simply by getting the salesperson to write their name on the brochures - 'John's copy not to be removed!' They explained that they weren't normally allowed to give out the catalogue – 'but I will for you because you are such a nice person'! They still lost them occasionally but not nearly as often.

Another car dealer said to me they had a problem in their service department with cheques bouncing. For younger readers cheques are pieces of paper that banks exchange for money! The law prevents garages from keeping your car (called lien) until the bill is paid.

Here is how we solved this problem. The receptionist would say 'I need to get the approval of the Service Manager to accept a cheque'. They would then walk out of the reception area and come back saying 'I can't find the service manager but I am sure you won't get me in trouble so I will break the rules just for you!' If there were a problem prospects would admit to it here.

The receptionists had to be aware of people saying yes and meaning no. When people agree with you they answer quickly and upgrade what you say. When disagreeing they hesitate and downgrade what you say. For example I say 'that's a nice carpet isn't it?' People agreeing will respond 'Yes, isn't it lovely'. Notice they have upgraded nice to lovely. If they disagree the response will have a hesitation and sound something like 'yeeessss it is ok'. Notice they have downgraded nice to OK. Both seem to be agreeing but one is definitely not.

When I first suggested referring to the service manager the dealer told me that they had tried that and service managers were no better at spotting dud cheques than service receptionists. It was only when we put in a bit of reciprocation (that the service receptionist couldn't find the sales manager but would break the rules just for them) that the technique worked.

Some examples of things to offer:

Visits to the prospect's home or business

Getting stock

Opening boxes to let the prospect see the product

Getting stock from another branch

Calling a manufacturer to get more information

Arranging an time to let them know an answer to their questions.

Arranging a demonstration of software etc.

These can all be used to invoke the need to reciprocate. If the prospect refuses to allow you to go to any trouble then the chances are they have a hidden objection.

The question is what to do about hidden objections if you can't ask questions! If the prospect won't tell you what their objection is, then the only option is to create an objection. The easiest objection to create is a price objection. Before using this strategy make sure you are comfortable handling price objections!

To create an objection go through this with the 'Dove':

'You know in my experience there are only three reasons people don't buy from me'. If you are uncomfortable with this change the words and retain the concept. For example 'my boss always says there are only three reasons prospects don't buy from us'.

You need to pause here and wait for some indication you should carry on. Because of the way intrigue works no one will guess what the three reasons are. You probably aren't guessing now, you are simply reading on!

The first is if they don't like me! And I understand that, I wouldn't buy from someone I don't like! Again you can change the words if you are uncomfortable. 'You have had a bad experience with our company before and I understand that'. Change the words but retain the concept for example 'you don't like our stock availability'. Recently I worked with jewellers who were much more comfortable saying 'you don't like the materials I work with'.

Again you need silence here until the prospect confirms that it is not you, your company or whatever you have chosen to use!

'The second reason is if they don't like the product or our brands and I can understand that, I wouldn't buy something I didn't like'.

Again you may need silence here until the prospect confirms that it is not the product. You may have to ask a question here to get them to commit to the product being suitable for them.

'Then that only leaves the third reason' – it's the price, it's a little too expensive isn't it'.

If you decide to use this then I will go through this carefully because if you don't use this technique in exactly the way that I have described it will fail.

You must go through the reasons one by one and get confirmation at each stage. This is because you are not telling the whole truth – there are far more than three reasons that people don't buy! I know I may offend some people here who may say this is unethical. There is no other effective way of exposing hidden objections. Questions may work occasionally but are seen as pressure. The alternative is to give up and lose the potential sale.

The value of using the technique is to close escape routes. Selling has been likened to leading a prospect down a corridor. All the way down the corridor there are open escape doors. Your job is to close each door as you approach it and lead the prospect to the sale at the end.

When you use the technique the way I have described you are closing the escape routes.

If you say to a prospect, 'you know there are only three reason people don't buy from me, it is either me, the product or the price, which is it? You will fail. The prospect will simply repeat their previous statement e.g. 'no, it's none of these, I simply want to think about it'.

When you say, 'you know in my experience there are only three reasons people don't buy from me', you must pause for an answer. If the prospect answers it means that they have implicitly accepted that there are only three reasons people don't buy.

'The first is if they don't like me! And I understand that, I wouldn't buy from someone I don't like!'

People never say it is because they don't like you. Not to me anyway!!!

'The second reason is if they don't like the product and I can understand that, I wouldn't buy something I didn't like'.

People usually say the product is great. If they don't then you have your objection (it's the product) and you have achieved your objective, which was to create an objection. You should now move on to handling the real objection.

'Then that only leaves the third reason – it's the price, it's a little too expensive isn't it'.

At this point, provided you stay quiet, the prospect will either say:

'Yes'   or

'No, it's not that, it's just .....' and then they will go on to explain the real objection

In any objection the second thing that people say is generally more truthful than the first thing they say.

You now have your objection and you can move on to handling it.

When running courses some people feel this is a pressure technique and feel uncomfortable about trying it. I understand that, anything new may feel uncomfortable. Change the words so that you can feel as comfortable as possible.

Others on courses give me examples of what they do. In almost every occasion their suggestions are to put the customer under some pressure. For example people say; ask questions to find out what the real objection is. That is pressure. If someone says 'I need to think about it' asking questions will be seen as pressurising by the prospect.

Offering discounts, free delivery or other techniques are seen as pressure. I am not saying these techniques are bad, if they work then use them. What I am saying is that before you put people under any pressure you should use reciprocity to make sure you are putting the right people under pressure (those with a hidden objection) rather than genuine potential buyers.

Almost everyone has had the experience of feeling pressured when they were genuinely thinking about buying something. Most of us have, at least once, decided against buying simply because of that pressure.

Detail or Overview?
Stick to overview. Easily done if you have established the correct rapport. I am sure you have said to a friend, 'it's complicated, leave that to me I'll sort it for you!'

Should you prepare an agenda for a meeting, if so why?
Yes (see the 'Eagle') but don't expect an agenda to be followed!

How do these people react when things go wrong?
Sometimes they go to 'Eagle' simply because they are upset at being put in this position. Often they can blame themselves and you need to be careful to prevent that.

What added value is a good salesperson for this prospect?
A good trusted friend.

Spending time with them, not hurrying them along too much, taking care of the details for them, solving any issues and being a regular point of contact. I once met a car salesperson that wouldn't let any of his customers speak to anyone else in the dealership. He was their only contact. He would organise services, repairs everything. Other car salespeople said to him that they didn't have time to do all that. He said he didn't have time to prospect! He had the most loyal prospect base I have ever seen.

The signal that identifies someone behaving as a 'Dove':
Easy, whenever I have a prospect not objecting and still not buying I fly straight into reciprocity. You may have had other signals earlier and none of them matter. It is only when things are going wrong that you need to take action.

'Peacock'
Advice if the prospect is behaving as a 'Peacock'

Questioning
The 'Peacock' needs a mixture of all types of questions. Never too much of anything, ask some fact questions, some opinions, some past and some future questions.

Would you use 'small talk' to warm up these prospects?
Some but not too much, be guided by them. Don't waste their time by your small talk. Better to listen to their holiday story than tell them yours. Be particularly careful with 'topping' their stories. They had a holiday – you had a better one. They broke their leg - you had a worse break etc.

Interrupting
Ok to interrupt occasionally don't overuse it though.

If they are wrong it is better to interrupt them and nip it in the bud. Always allow them to save face in the same way as the 'Eagle'.

Short Gaps in the Conversation
See the 'Eagle' answer.

Your Opinion
Not too often and only if it is right and valuable! Always back it up by including the word 'because'.

Loyalty and Price Sensitivity
This is the prospect that is both Loyal and Price Sensitive. This is the negotiator. This prospect will tell you that they have a better price from a competitor.

This is the signal that I am dealing with a 'Peacock'. It comes down to a negotiation. I will deal with this in more detail in the chapter on negotiation but for now understand the implications of someone telling you they have a better price. What is implied is that they want to buy it **from you!** If they didn't want to buy it from you they wouldn't be talking to you - they would be buying it from the lower priced supplier.

One of the roles of the salesperson is to make the implied explicit and the explicit implied. This is exactly the case here and so the first thing you need to make explicit is that they do want to buy it from you.

Ask them 'Who would you prefer to buy from?'

If you ask this question you will only ever get two answers:

'From You'

or

'I don't mind; I'll buy it from the cheapest'

No one will ever say I would prefer to buy from your competitor because, if they did, that's where they would be.

The route you take depends on which answer they give:

From you

Ask them 'Why?'. Before you do though make sure you disguise the word. For example you could say 'It is really important for us to understand what is important to you. Would you mind if I asked you why you would prefer to buy from us'. You could ask 'Why?' avoiding the word altogether. For example 'How come? What do we do that is important to you?'

Anything they say negates their ability to negotiate.

Bear in mind the first law of business. Out of the three words:

Fast

Good

Cheap

It is only possible to provide two from the three.

Fast and good cannot be cheap

Fast and cheap cannot be good

Good and cheap cannot be fast

There is a cost to fast and good. To be fast and good you need to have stock, (costs money) lots of locations, (costs money) staff, (costs money) and quality products (costs money). The cost of being fast and good prohibits being cheap.

 Most businesses understand this. Usually I would then have a conversation about the prospects own business. What two do they focus on? Often prospects will say they <u>try</u> to be fast, good and cheap. So do I and I know it is impossible. I have never met any customer that actually thinks they are the cheapest supplier in their industry, it is something that all businesses have to grapple with.

Now you need to explain that being fast and good saves money. We do this by explaining the difference between price and cost, which I will cover in the next section.

I don't mind, I'll buy from the cheapest

Again you need to make explicit that the lowest price is not necessarily the cheapest. You can do this by asking 'is it the price or cost that concerns you?' Typically when I use this I would extend this by saying 'perhaps I should explain what I mean by the price and the cost'.

The price is the amount you pay in the short term. The cost is how much it costs you in total.

For example if you are a tradesman charging £20 per hour. You buy something for £20 and it takes you one hour to drive to the merchants. The cost to you is £40.

I have always wondered about this with supermarkets. I go to a supermarket to buy groceries. It takes me 30 minutes to drive there. I use a gallon of petrol, which costs me £6, and I add 40 miles depreciation on the car. I spend one hour in the supermarket. 30 minutes to drive back and I save £10!!! Where is the logic in that??

The price is lower and the cost is higher.

If I buy a piece of furniture for £500 and because it is low quality I have to replace it in four years with another at £500 the cost is £1000 compared with £750 to buy better quality in the first place. Typically it would be replaced by the more expensive one and so the real cost is now £1250 for the lower priced route.

So being fast and good saves money for the prospect. If the supplier focussed on being cheap the customers would lose money either because they weren't good or they weren't fast.

When I use this technique I would always use it with the following value quotations.

'Buying cheap can cost you dearly'

'You only get what you pay for'

'The bitterness of poor quality lingers long after the sweet taste of low price is forgotten'

'It is unwise to pay too much but it is more unwise to pay too little. If you pay too much you only loose a little money. If you pay too little then you run the risk of losing everything'.

It is worthwhile spending a little time in your business to work out what are the four most important ways that you save money for customers even though you charge a higher price.

Detail or Overview?
A detailed overview!

Should you prepare an agenda for a meeting, if so why?
Yes (see the 'Eagle').

How do these people react when things go wrong?
Usually ok. Sort it out and they will be happy.

What added value is a good salesperson for this prospect?
Someone who will admire them. Shower them with plenty of (genuine) praise. Catch them doing things right and compliment them.

Always be busy. Your time is a scarce resource, once passed it can never be recovered. Make appointments and phone beforehand to say you are on your way. It is better to have an appointment cancelled over the phone that when you arrive.

The signal that identifies someone behaving as a 'Peacock':

The signal you are dealing with a 'Peacock' is a negotiation. It is a different style of negotiation than with an 'Eagle'. With the 'Peacock' everything was going well, you are getting a sale then suddenly at the very end - a request for discount. It is usually done in a very friendly way.

DECISION INFLUENCERS

There are three different types of decision influencers in an account:

The Economic buyer
Usually the purchasing manager but it could be the owner. They hold the purse strings; they can say 'no' but can't say 'yes'. They may decide where to buy but they cannot decide what to buy. If you approach them with a new product they would need to refer to others. Often salespeople see them, wrongly, as the most important person in a prospect account.

The Technical Buyer
It could be the Architect, Engineer, Design or IT team. They specify what the product must have and what the product can't have. If you were trying to substitute your preferred brand they would be the people that have to agree to it.

User Buyer
It could be the person that installs or uses the product or service. In a larger company it is more likely to be the production engineer or site foreman. It is the person that depends on your service levels. If a delivery is late this is the person that is affected by it. If a product fails they have to sort out the problem.

In the following exercise consider what is important to the different buyers and rank them in order of importance.

The four factors that may be important are:

P = Price

C = Convenience – How easy is it to deal with you, your service levels, do they have an account? Is your literature and website user friendly?

F = Features – Facts about the product

B = Benefits – Your opinion about what the feature does for them

Rank what is important for each buyer type:

(1 = Most important, 4 = Less important)

Economic Buyer

1	2	3	4

Technical Buyer

1	2	3	4

User Buyer

1	2	3	4

Confirmation Bias may have affected your answers! Let's look at the evidence.

Economic Buyer

1	2	3	4
C	P	B	F

Convenience is the most important thing to an economic buyer but they may perceive that Price is the most important thing. Convenience is the emotional driver and price is the logical answer. The secret is to appeal to the real motivator (Convenience) and avoid objections about the perceived motivator (Price).

This means if you asked an economic buyer: 'what do we need to do to get your business?' they will usually answer 'Price'. Therefore this is a very bad question!

You cannot simply tell an economic buyer that what drives their behaviour is principally convenience and then price. Sell the convenience before the price is discussed.

The evidence that Convenience is the most important motivator:

Reduction of suppliers
It is usually the purchasing department that want to reduce the number of suppliers.

Usually one supplier
Generally, when a purchasing department are getting quotes for multiple lines they will want to place the business with one supplier. Very few purchasing departments use ten suppliers when they could use one.

Opening an account
It is usually difficult to get a purchasing department to open a new account.

Preferred supplier
It is actually unusual for a purchasing department to change suppliers. That is why they will use lower quotes as a negotiation tool with the preferred supplier.

Now brainstorm what you could do to improve 'convenience' for economic buyers?

Some things you may consider:

One stop shopping
- Wide product range

- Specially sourced products that are not SKUs (Stock Keeping Units)

- Help with tenders

Website

- User friendly web site

- Visibility of prices

- Market pricing rather than list or recommended pricing

- Online invoicing

- Email orders and payments online

- Regular products in a shopping list format

- Most popular products

- Product search

- Product comparison

- Project management system

Pricing
- Consistent pricing

- Customised pricing

- Locked in prices

- Price rise notifications

Communication
- Integrated IT systems

- Consolidated invoices to reduce the number of invoices

- Communicate directly with other departments to avoid purchasing having to chase up orders

- One point of contact

- Quick quote process

- Quote follow up service

Accounting
- Accurate invoicing and statement reconciliation

Features are the least important for the economic buyer because whilst the salesperson is bleating on about more features the economic buyer is thinking: costs more, breaks down, more complex etc. Avoid discussing features with economic buyers. The interesting thing about this is that whenever a salesperson gets a price objection from an economic buyer they are most likely to combat this with features!

If you feel the need to talk to a buyer have the technical buyer or user buyer with you. If that isn't possible use their credibility e.g. 'the architect said they wanted xxx'.

You need to avoid talking to economic buyers about things that have no interest for them. It may be that your company's USPs (Unique Selling Points) are number of branches, product quality, after-sales etc. but these things are usually of no interest to the economic buyer.

It is also interesting how many presentations from prospective suppliers start off with exactly these i.e. number of branches, length of time in business etc.

Technical Buyer

1	2	3	4
C	F	B	P

Convenience is the most important thing to a technical buyer but they may perceive that Features are the most important thing. Convenience is the emotional driver and features are the logical answer. The secret is to appeal to the real motivator (Convenience) and avoid objections about the perceived motivator (Features).

This means if you ask a technical buyer: 'what do we need to do to win your business?' they will usually answer 'great products with the best features'. This is still a bad question!

You cannot simply tell a technical buyer that what drives their behaviour is principally convenience not features. You need to sell the convenience aspect of your business before discussing products and features.

Start by doing a presentation on your website. Remember how many different websites there are, each organised slightly differently. Show technical buyers how to find technical details as well as MSDS (Material Safety Data Sheets) etc.

The evidence that Convenience is the most important motivator:

Preferred catalogue

Probably not as easy to see as they move to web based catalogues but the same principle applies with web-based catalogues as with paper catalogues. How many catalogues would the average architect have in their office? Hundreds! How many will they actually use - only one or two? Could it be that a few catalogues contain the best products with the best features? No, of course it isn't. It is because architects get used to looking up information in the catalogues they are familiar with. The secret is to become the 'catalogue of choice'.

The same applies to websites. Architects, specifiers and engineers won't take time to study your website. You need to statistically analyse what happens on your website when an architect or engineer uses it. How long do they spend looking at each page — where are the roadblock pages?

Discontinued products

How many construction projects have discontinued products specified? The answer is most. The biggest construction project in Australia, the new Adelaide Hospital, was entirely specified with discontinued plumbing products!

Is that because these products have the best features? No, of course not. It is because it is easier to cut and paste from previous projects.

Unless you can get an Architect to cut and paste from your site you can't get specified.

Now brainstorm what you could do to improve 'convenience' for technical buyers?

Some things you may consider:

Website
- Product specifications

- Cut & paste

- Online planners

- Product comparisons

- Material Safety Data Sheets (MSDS)

- Sustainability information

- Online training

Guides
- Selector guides

- Set out guides

Products
- New product alerts

- Trend notifications

- Product trainers

- Samples

- Product range

The reason price is the least important here is that prices given to an architect are usually preliminary indications. The price given to an architect will generally be higher than a price given to anyone else. How does that help your product to be specified? This is why I recommend using a 'Market Price' system rather than 'Retail' or 'List' pricing system.

User Buyer

1	2	3	4
C	B	F	P

Convenience is the most important thing to a user buyer but they may perceive that Benefits are the most important thing. Convenience is the emotional driver and benefits are the logical answer. The secret is to appeal to the real motivator (Convenience) and avoid objections about the perceived motivator (Benefits).

Unusually if you ask a user buyer: 'what do we need to do to win your business?' they will often answer in terms of pricing. I have no idea why this is. Pricing isn't even a perceived motivator. Perhaps they reply to the question they think you are asking, 'what do we need to do to get your buyer to buy from us'. This is still a bad question!

You cannot simply tell a technical buyer that what drives their behaviour is principally convenience not features.

The evidence that Convenience is the most important motivator:

Location

A user buyer would rarely drive past an open supplier to get to another one. They usually go to the closest supplier.

An account

User buyers will go where they have an account.

Some companies have a credit card they give to user buyers so that if they don't have an account they can still buy unusual things needed to complete a job. They would still go to where they have an account first.

Relationship

User buyers will go where they are known and get better service.

Staff knowledge

User buyers will avoid suppliers they perceive lack knowledge about their business — the point being it takes longer to get what you need.

Now brainstorm what could you do to improve 'convenience' for user buyers?

Some things you may consider:

- Locations

- Deliveries

- Staff expertise

- Product training sessions

- Design departments

Price is the least important thing for a user buyer, which is why dockets given to user buyers aren't normally priced. Normally they wouldn't know the prices you are charging their company. They may be told not to use a company 'because they are too expensive'. Avoid discussing prices with user buyers.

It is interesting that economic buyers are often perceived as the most important people in an account when actually it is the users that are most important. If there is a dispute between economic buyers and user buyers then the users will always win (eventually). Keep working hard with both groups and recognise when the economic buyer has a change of heart it is almost always because of the pressure from the user buyers.

⊙PTIMIST ⊙R PESSIMIST

I always wondered what type of person bought a product because you would fix it if it broke down. I once read a mystery shop report, the shopper said; 'the salesperson explained all about the guarantee but when I thought about it I didn't much like the idea of my appliance breaking down'.

After that I started looking carefully at what type of people like guarantees. It led me to a whole new strategy.

I found that optimists and pessimists are interested in different things.

Optimists are excited by the words:

New

Exclusive

Exciting

Trial offer

End of Line

Increase

Improve

Gain

Pessimists are motivated more easily using:

Guaranteed

Brand names

Most popular

Savings

Reductions

How do you tell optimists and pessimists apart? Very easily, optimists will tend to point out what they like when you are presenting products. Pessimists will tend to point out what they don't like.

When presenting to optimists you should mention the guarantee and not make a big thing of it. You may think that saying you have a five-year guarantee implies better quality. You are right and you are also confirming the product does indeed break down.

When presenting to pessimists you should mention the stability and popularity of the product. If you have a new and exciting product you may wish to stress the size and quality of the manufacturer.

End of line is an interesting one. The end of line can be presented as tried and tested technology. It can also be presented as out of date with spares being a difficulty. You can put the slant based on the product and your objectives.

RELATIONSHIP SELLING

I work with some Private Banks. Their target prospects vary depending on the bank. Usually they are looking for individuals with a minimum of £2 million liquid investments. With some banks their target is people with over £50 million in assets.

When I talk about Confirmation Bias with them I am amazed at how many think that price or interest rates or exchange rates is 100% of the decision to buy. They think billionaires pay them for banking when I get it for free but price is the most important thing! They ignore the additional services that their customers expect.

If I want to call my bank manager I have to wait until the branch opens. Private bankers are available 24/7!

After we discuss Confirmation Bias and start focusing on the real motivation for buying, they think the single most important thing is relationships. Relationships are important but it is a business relationship based on value that is important, not a social relationship.

When salespeople think that relationship is the most important thing they tend to ask personal questions to try to develop a social relationship with prospects. They try to find out about hobbies, children etc. When I am buying something, whether it is financial advice or a product, I am looking for expertise not a new best friend! Salespeople focussing on developing a personal relationship are focussing on their needs not on the prospects needs.

How many of your customers would you invite to your daughter's wedding? Most customer relationships are purely business relationships based on value. I have made lots of friends through business but when I move on, or they move on, the relationship closes.

I know some Private Banker's prospects move with them when they go to another bank and it is also true that most don't. If prospects move with the salesperson it is usually because of a failure on the part of the current provider.

If my insurance broker, lawyer or accountant left their company and the replacement contacted me quickly enough I would give the company a chance. The trouble is most company's contact the customer to say: 'X has left and we will contact you again, soon, to let you know what action we are going to take'. This implies they are really busy with other, more important, clients. They will get to you someday!'

If an employee is leaving, contact and visit your prospect **immediately**. If you do this there is a well-known psychological principle that says: 'in uncertainty, people do nothing'. If you work hard at it most people will stay.

If a prospect moves with the salesperson they are generally not moving because of the relationship alone. If that were the case then relationship managers could leave the bank and be self-employed working from an office in their own home. If prospects were moving because of the relationship then there would be no need to move to another firm.

In fact I have found the hardest people to sell to are my closest friends. They can object without even making sense! People don't buy from you just because you are a great person; they buy from you because you provide value.

Your relationship with your prospects should be based on providing value, not on being a nice person. My rule is to make friends with customers, not make customers of friends. Divorce business contacts from social occasions. If you meet a prospect at a social event, make an appointment to see them in a business setting as quickly as possible.

There is some research which suggests that liking does play a positive role in rapport and trust and therefore improves selling. The subtle factor that is often overlooked in this research is that salespeople were asked to disclose personal information not ask personal questions.

I don't have to like the people that sell to me but it sure helps.

SECTION THREE
SELLING SKILLS

AMBIENCE

Music

Would you believe that the music you play in a retail setting can dramatically influence your sales?

A study conducted in a wine merchants:

They played French music and had a special offer on French wines. Sales of French wines outsold sales of German wines by 3 to 1.

Next they played German music and put an offer on German wines. This time German wines outsold French wines by 2 to 1. Not such a pronounced effect but nonetheless a positive result.

Then they played classical music and found that whilst it didn't affect the promotion sales the price of the average bottle sold went up. People listening to classical music were prepared to spend more per bottle.

Finally they played Italian music and the sales went down and one prospect threatened violence to the manager if they didn't turn down the music!

There are strong correlations between:

- The speed we walk at and

- The music we are listening to

Also between:

- The time spent in a shop and

- Buying from that shop

Therefore the best advice is to play slow music (not Italian!)

Dress code

Suits or polo shirts? Definitely a trend towards more casual wear.

Probably depends on the business but there is no doubt that customers want to be able to easily differentiate between staff and other customers.

THE APPROACH AND
INTRODUCTION

I find it amazing that in the 30+ years I have been in selling the worst phrases to use with prospects are still regularly used!

In retail selling it is:

> 'How may I help you?' or 'can I help you?'

In business selling it is:

> 'How's business?'

So how about approaching prospects differently?

Any approach should be:

- Intriguing

- Novel or

- Surprising

My favourite introduction in retail selling is 'the choice is amazing nowadays isn't it'. The implied statement here is that they need an expert to help them through the maze of choice. They are lucky because they have an expert standing right next to them!

In business how about 'I have another meeting scheduled for 1pm is that ok?' You wouldn't use this right at the beginning but could fairly soon after. The implied statement is 'I won't be wasting your time today'!

When should you approach people in a showroom or shop? Whenever they touch something. They must be looking for some information, at least about the feel of the product, at that time.

When people enter a showroom, looking for brochures and leave without one they rarely come back. I mentioned reciprocation earlier and the most common form of reciprocation is to give brochures to people.

The rules of engagement are:

- Smile

- Use positive language

- Adopt an air of success

- Use humour (if you are a funny person!)

- Use positive labels for prospects

In terms of body language if you adopt the right attitude then you can follow your natural inclination. I talked earlier about labels, if we give nice labels to prospects our body language will be congruent with that label.

One area that some people need help with is eye contact. Let me start by saying that direct eye-to-eye contact is either an aggressive gesture or a signal that people are very much in love. If you are not in love with your prospect then don't think staring them directly in the eyes will help!

In a study, about telling lies, researchers found that even children as young as three years old made eye contact when lying. Beware of excessive eye contact.

Normally we don't look people directly, in the eyes, we actually lip-read. You can tell this by how annoying it is watching a film that is dubbed or the sound is slightly out of sync. It is also evident when the person you are talking to has some lunch left on a tooth!

What happens is that, whilst I am speaking to you, I will watch your eyes and you will watch my lips. I am gauging your reaction and you are lip-reading. When you speak I am watching your lips and you are now watching my eyes. Our eyes are only in direct contact fleetingly. Try this and you will find eye contact a lot easier.

Research found that there might be a downside! If the speaker watches the lips of the listener it may be read as a signal that you want to kiss them!

QUESTIONING

I have already mentioned the myth of open and closed questions. Having said this we do need to understand the needs, wants, values, beliefs and opinions of prospects in order to sell to them effectively.

I discovered that questions asked by a salesperson could come from two different directions. They can either be questions that the answers will help the salesperson to sell, or questions that help them to understand the needs of the prospect.

I do an exercise on courses to illustrate this.

I find someone in the audience who has a fear of something. Let's say I have a volunteer who has a fear of water. I will refer to this volunteer as the 'Fear Volunteer'.

I ask them to sit in the middle of the room.

I then ask for a volunteer who loves scuba diving. When I get a volunteer I ask them what their hobbies are and what is a perfect weekend for them to win as a prize. I will refer to this volunteer as the 'Selling Volunteer'.

We now have a 'fear volunteer' who has a fear of water. We also have a 'selling volunteer' that loves scuba diving and a perfect weekend for them would be to watch a major football cup final.

I offer an all expenses paid trip for the 'selling volunteer' and a partner, of their choice, to the UEFA cup final, which is next Wednesday. I check they are free to fly out on Wednesday and back Thursday or Friday. They usually are! I also offer £200 spending money.

All that they have to do to earn this fabulous trip is to get the other person on a diving trip this weekend. I have organised a boat and it leaves at two o'clock on Sunday. Can they persuade them to come on the trip?

Both participants have heard the briefing. They both know what each other are likely to do.

I will relate the typical approach:

Selling Volunteer:	What are you doing on Sunday?
Fear Volunteer:	I am busy visiting friends.
SV:	We have something fabulous lined up that I am sure you will enjoy. How would you like to come with us?
FV:	What is it?
SV:	Well it is a life changing experience that you will really enjoy.
FV:	Is it dangerous?
SV:	No, no it is perfectly safe.
FV:	What do I have to do?
SV:	Nothing you just have to come out with us and enjoy the day.

FV: When you say out what do you mean?

SV: Do you like boats?

FV: Yes I don't mind boats provided they are quite big and it is not too rough and I don't need to go near water.

SV: Oh no this boat is very big and I am sure it won't be rough on Sunday. I have checked the weather forecast and it is really good.

FV: OK then I might come with you.

SV: Have you ever wondered what it was like under the sea? The beautiful sights and the lovely fish. Do you like fish?

FV: Only on a plate!

SV: Underwater is really beautiful.

FV: Yes, but I don't like water.

SV: Why is that?

FV: I am just frightened of it. I get cold sweats when I think of it. I think .....

SV: Have you ever thought of confronting your fear?

FV: I have tried many times and every time it fails.

SV: Why has it failed?

FV: I am frightened I am going to drown.

SV: So if I could get it really safe and in fact if the boat didn't go out very far. In fact you don't even need to go out of your depth do you? (They then ask me – 'you didn't say they had to be out of their depth did you?' I respond it is not a condition to be out of their depth)

FV: No I don't think so. What is in it for me?

SV: Well you get an opportunity to overcome your fear. Do you like football?

FV: Yes I do, why?

SV: If you did this you could come with me to see the UEFA cup final.

FV: No thanks.

SV: What if I gave you £100 spending money and all expenses paid?

FV: No I'm not interested.

The strategy that the 'selling volunteer' followed here is the strategy I think people naturally follow to sell something if they haven't been trained to sell. Let me break it down.

Step No 1

They go for a close at the beginning:

SV   What are you doing on Sunday?

This is a failure strategy. The suspicion and distrust that is built up here makes it very difficult to sell. The equivalent in selling is to ask:

'Do you buy new products as soon as they hit the market?'

or

'Do you use ..... product?'

If you ask questions like these don't be surprised if people don't tell you the truth.

Fear Volunteer: I am busy visiting friends.

If someone doesn't tell you the truth then to me it is self evident they don't trust you. One of the ways to identify selling questions is people often do not tell the truth when answering them. That is where we get the expression 'buyers are liars'. It isn't because people are inherent liars. If you ask a question that people would be stupid to answer with the truth then expect them to lie.

Step No 2

They hide the true objective. This is one reason there is a trend towards titles such as consultants and designers rather than salespeople. The selling volunteer may exaggerate and possibly even start lying:

SV: We have something fabulous lined up that I am sure you will enjoy. How would you like to come with us?

FV: What is it?

SV: Well it is a life changing experience that you will really enjoy.

Step No 3

They get asked a difficult question and they answer with a lie!

FV: Is it dangerous?

SV: No, no it is perfectly safe.

FV: What do I have to do?

SV: Nothing you just have to come out with us and enjoy the day?

Step No 4

They 'sell the benefits':

SV: Have you ever wondered what it was like under the sea? The beautiful sights and the lovely fish. Do you like fish?

FV: Only on a plate!

SV: Underwater is really beautiful.

Step No 5

They ask 'Why?' at all the wrong times:

FV: Yes but I don't like water.

SV: Why is that?

Step No 6

They miss information by interrupting:

FV: I am just frightened of it. I get cold sweats when I think of it. I think .....

SV: Have you ever thought of confronting your fear?

Step No 7

They miss buying signals and don't use why at the right times. The right question now would be 'Why have you tried to confront your fear?'

FV: I have tried many times and every time it fails.

SV: Why has it failed?

FV: I am frightened I am going to drown.

Step No 8

Then they go back to closing using the 'if I could, would you' close:

| SV: | So if I could get it really safe and in fact if the boat didn't go out very far. In fact you don't even need to go out of your depth do you? |

Step No 9

And finally we get to bribery. It isn't that the 'fear volunteer' was price sensitive. The 'selling volunteer' encouraged them to be price sensitive because of their selling strategy:

FV:	No I don't think so. What is in it for me?
SV:	Well you get an opportunity to overcome your fear. Do you like football?
FV:	Yes I do, why?
SV:	If you did this you could come with me to see the UEFA cup final.

Using this approach a negotiation is an inevitable consequence of the strategy. Human beings all listen to the same radio station. It is called WIIFM (what's in it for me?). If you try to get someone to buy from you because it is in your (the sellers) interest then negotiation is an inevitable consequence.

It is helpful to consider here that people don't generally know what they need. The salesperson must help them to understand what they need and want. If you ask a direct question the answer will not be useful. For example 'How important is delivery to you?' The answer may be, 'very important', but that does not help the prospect place a value on that need. To do so you need to ask understanding questions to help them.

Returning to the exercise.

Usually the 'fear volunteer' is a little stressed at this stage. They normally want to speak about the fear and the 'selling volunteer' has prevented this from happening.

It takes me a little while to calm them down. I usually talk a little of my fear as well. I don't like being out of my depth in water when I can't see what else is in the water. I don't mind swimming pools but Liverpool Docks holds no attraction for me!

I then ask them about their fear. I have had some hairy stories on courses about people nearly drowning. Being pushed into harbours before they could swim. So called 'friends' terrifying the living daylights out of them. Often on the course other delegates (that have until now been solely observers) start to get interested in the story and start asking understanding questions.

I would like to keep them talking as long as I can to explore their feelings about what happened to them. I ask them about other situations – holidays etc. I ask them about friends and family. Do their children swim? How do they feel about that? Generally I am gaining an understanding of their fear.

Then I will look at the buying signal. 'You said you had tried many times to conquer it, why have you tried many times?' This is the correct use of 'Why?' as it is a positive situation. I want them to try again and so I always ask why they tried - never why did it fail?

They will now tell me that they are desperate to overcome their fear. They have tried many times because they see others enjoying themselves and they feel left out.

I can then introduce a potential solution. If my solution is attractive they will pay me to help them. I ask people how much they would pay for a solution and most answer that 'it depends'. Usually they are willing to pay something whereas previously they were resisting bribery.

In this way I can help someone's problems and get them to pay for it. I am not teaching them to be price sensitive I am teaching them the value of the solution. Any negotiation is based on how much extra they are prepared to pay rather than how much I have to bribe them with.

Of course fairy tales are easy in books. Sometimes the approach fails. Some people are happy with their fear and are desperate to hold on to it. In these cases we don't make a sale. My contention here is that my job is not to get a sale at any cost. That is short-term thinking. My job is simply to see if what I sell would be a beneficial purchase for the prospect. Do they need it and if so how much is it worth to them?

The process I use here is a completely different mind shift, away from selling, towards understanding. When I understand prospects I can discover if my product is of any value to them.

It is as simple as that. What you are selling is a by-product. If it happens to meet with the needs of your prospect you get a sale. If your product does not meet with the needs of your prospect you don't get a sale – and nor should you! If you get a sale in these circumstances you have either misled your prospect or misunderstood them. Either way you cannot get repeat business on this basis.

Some characteristics of Selling and Understanding questions.

Selling Questions

- Are leading e.g. 'were you happy with the response rate to your campaign?'

- You have a solution you have thought of before asking the question e.g. 'what do you think of the service you are getting from your current supplier?' If the prospect isn't happy the solution is to buy from you.

- There is a perfect answer as far as you are concerned e.g. 'what is your budget?' The perfect answer as far as you are concerned is 'I will spend whatever it takes to get what I want'.

- Prospects don't always answer truthfully i.e. all of the above!

- The answer is only for your benefit and so the prospect wouldn't lose anything if the question were never asked e.g. 'have you had any other quotations?'

- They are fact finding e.g. 'what is your buying level of authority?'

- They are commitment based e.g. 'if there was a product that did this for you would you buy it?'

Understanding Questions

- Although the question may be about the past the reason you are asking is to help future decisions e.g. 'what do you like about your existing product?'

- They are about the prospects values / beliefs / opinions e.g. 'what would be the three most important things for you to achieve in the next financial year?'

- They address any concerns the prospect may have e.g. 'what would you see as the biggest obstacle to a successful product launch?' Prospects almost always answer truthfully.

- They are asked only for the benefit of the prospect to make sure that no mistakes are made in suggesting the wrong product or service.

- There is no commitment to buy implied by answering the question.

- They are 'nice to know' questions rather than 'need to know' questions.

Note:

The distinction between the types of questions is not clear-cut. The determining factor being, whether the question is being asked because it helps you to sell, or to determine the right product for the prospect. This is why it is not a clear distinction because selecting the right product obviously makes it easier to sell.

If there is any doubt in the prospect's mind they sometimes ask 'Why do you want to know that?' To avoid this explain your reason for asking a question before asking it.

'Understanding Questions' are:

- Much better at highlighting pain

- Better for developing trust and rapport

If you can identify a pain in a prospect's business you are much more likely to overcome the 'habit' and 'regret' pressure the buyer experiences.

The good news is if we look back at things that are more important than price in the decision to buy how many of your prospects haven't experienced 'pain' in their business.

How many prospects haven't:

- Suffered from poor product quality?

- Suffered from lack of stock at their supplier?

- Suffered from a late delivery?

- Suffered from poor after sales service?

- Suffered from poor sales service?

- Suffered from inconsistent pricing?

- Suffered from poor paperwork?

- Suffered from wrong invoicing?

- Suffered from not being able to speak to the right person in a supplier?

- Suffered from lack of knowledge in a supplier?

Any one of these may be enough to overcome a price objection if the sale is handled properly and I don't know many businesses that haven't suffered from every one of these.

The problem is getting customers to tell the salesperson that these things happen and the impact on their business when these happen. The solution is generally by complimenting the existing suppliers (reverse psychology) and asking understanding questions. When you have found the 'pain' then it is relatively easy to build up that pain so that you are in a position to overcome price objections. Remember pain is emotional - price is logical.

Given that you now have the tools to avoid or overcome any objections all that remains is to use that information effectively.

PROPOSING SOLUTIONS

In the absence of any difference between two options people will choose the lowest price. Your job as a salesperson is to show that there is a differentiation between the two options and that the differences are worth any additional cost.

When proposing solutions the objective is to create four differentiators. One problem is how many salespeople say there is less differentiation between products today and that they are selling a commodity. I find that incredible.

One dictionary definition of a commodity is 'a class of goods for which there is demand, but which is supplied without qualitative differentiation across a market'.

I rarely find that customers consider products as having absolutely no qualitative difference. Most tradesmen have their favourite brands for one reason or another. Many motorists think there is a qualitative difference between BP, Shell and Esso petrol.

I am going to repeat the definition of commodity: 'a class of goods for which there is demand, but which is supplied without qualitative differentiation across a market'.

No 'qualitative differentiation'.

In America, by law, vodka must be colourless, tasteless and as odourless (spelling changed) as possible. It is the same vodka as sold in Britain but people here tell me they can smell and taste vodka.

It must therefore be a commodity? If you look at the success of vodka there is a lesson in differentiation.

Smirnoff (£17) was the biggest selling brand of vodka. Then came Absolut (£20); they created a new 'premium vodka' category. Absolut took over as the biggest selling vodka. Then Blue Ice (USA No.1 in 2003 – not sold in UK) and Grey Goose (£59) created new super premium categories.

Between £17 and £59 for liquid that is colourless, almost odourless and tasteless by law!

Create your own differentiation. Compete where others are not trying to compete. Describe your business and your products in a way that implies differentiation. Avoid being compared to competitors. Everything you do is different.

I was asked by a prospect 'who would you consider to be your biggest competitor?' I thought it was a good question. My answer was 'do you mean in terms of quality or in terms of price?' My answer implied we didn't have a competitor that was both.

What I have found is that salespeople decide what they are selling is a commodity much quicker than the prospects. I can understand how this happens.

If you are an electrical supplier, every day you see these products. You don't use them and don't hear about it every time there is an issue (for example, you only hear of a fault when you sold it, not when your competitors sold it). You don't hear of issues with brands you don't sell. When there is an issue it is often long after the product was sold and so there is a memory gap.

Talk to existing loyal customers who buy the more expensive brand and they will usually give you information about the different brands and the differences between them.

All product differences should be explained using **FAB model**:

- Features

- Advantages

- Benefits

Features
A feature is a fact that very few people would disagree with. A car has four wheels. This car has ABS braking system. This car has airbags for the driver and passengers.

Advantage
This is an explanation of the feature and how it works. Why did the designer put it in the product in the first place? The four wheels make the car more stable on the road.

The ABS braking system eases off the power to wheels that are skidding.

Airbags inflate in certain serious accidents to prevent injury.

You will by now probably have worked out I am not an expert in cars! I use them as an example because most readers are familiar with cars. When I was writing this I was thinking I am not certain I could really give an accurate description of ABS!

Benefits

Benefits are opinions. They are what you think they will do for the prospect. As opinions some people can, and some will, disagree. Also, as opinions, some prospects don't want to hear what you think.

My opinion of ABS may be that it makes it safer for drivers. Some people would disagree with this. I understand that when a car is driving in a straight line on a dry surface your stopping distance correlates with the amount of rubber you leave on the road! Since ABS reduces this then in certain conditions ABS is less safe. It depends on your driving and the road conditions. Some modern cars allow the driver to switch off the ABS.

When presenting to these prospects ask them a question about the benefits. For example, 'this car has ABS braking that eases off the power to wheels that are skidding, how do you think that would help you?'

Another technique would be to say why the designers included the feature. For example:

The ABS braking system eases off the power to the wheels. The designers definitely needed to make it less likely a car would skid and needed to give more control of the car to the driver .

You could also use the word 'because' as in; 'the driver has more control of this car because it has ABS braking, which eases off the power to wheels that are skidding'.

Features and benefits can be:

Standard

Company

Differentiators

Standard

A standard feature is one that appears on every product in this class. People in general do not decide to buy on the basis of Standard Features. Don't make a big thing about standard features when selling.

When selling a car for example I would mention the features that are standard saying 'It has all the features you would expect from a car of this class including …..'

If they are standard features you can't afford to give the advantages and benefits of each one. If the prospect shops around, they would get bored very quickly if everyone explained everything.

If you keep your ears open you will sometimes get the opportunity to mention the advantages and benefits of Standard features. You should always offer to explain how they work, if the prospect wants to know.

Company

A company feature and benefit is associated to the company e.g. Ford have been in business for over 100 years.

Only mention these company features to pessimists.

Differentiators

The real reason people buy your product, or buy it from you, is that they see some differentiation. In essence they feel that what you are offering them is something different from what others offer.

The confusing part is that a differentiator could be a Standard or a Company Feature. For example Volvo chose to make safety their differentiation. The thing I remember about Volvo ads was the SIPS (Side Impact Protection System). Was that a differentiator? No absolutely not. Almost every car in that class had a side impact protection system. Were Volvo the first to have one? I am told it was SAAB that invented the Side Impact Protection System.

How was it a differentiator then?

A differentiator is something you major on that other people are ignoring. Volvo chose safety because everyone else was focussing on something else. At that time it was estimated that only 4% of car advertising mentioned safety.

What others are ignoring is as critical as you majoring on it to create a differentiator. Find out what your competitors are saying to prospects by mystery shopping them so you can identify your differences.

Of course some products do have real differentiation. That makes it a little easier. In most markets however the difference between products is becoming less. Sometimes, when running a course, delegates will tell me there is no difference between their products and their competitors. They are selling exactly the same product and even the same brand as their competitor.

So far I have only been talking about differentiation through products!

When doing a follow up sales training course I usually start with a slide explaining the role of a salesperson:

'To help the prospect to perceive value in the Services, Systems and Products'

I say to the delegates that when salespeople are differentiating they will almost always resort to the products for differentiation, what the product is made of, who makes it, where it's made or the product quality.

I will then remind them what I think about the importance of price in the decision to buy. I will say: 'If we are faced with a decision between buying two things and everything is exactly the same in all respects then I will go for the cheaper one.'

Then I ask them how often what they are selling is exactly the same in all respects as what their competitors sell. Amazingly even minutes after showing them the slide about services and systems the vast majority immediately think of products.

How often is what you are selling **exactly** the same as your competitors?

If you didn't answer 'NEVER' then you are only thinking about products.

Interestingly when you talk to customers you get the opposite reaction. When a customer asks for one of your exclusive products have some fun. Tell them it is an exclusive product and therefore because they cannot buy the same thing anywhere else you can make more profit on it!

My bet is your customer would tell you they won't buy it and that they can get 'exactly the same' from any supplier. It may not have the same label but it does the same job.

I am suggesting doing this as a joke – please don't do this!

185

Customers, in general, don't believe products to be exclusive.

100% of your prospects know absolutely that your services and systems are exclusive to you.

If you asked any prospect, do you think our competitors have access to our stock? Do you think they use our after-sales service? Do you think they use our invoicing and accounts departments? Do you think they use our product knowledge and expertise? How about our delivery system? Our network? Customers know your services and systems are unique but salespeople have difficulty selling the value of it.

Customers, in general, don't believe that your products are exclusive but salespeople rely on them and often ignore service differentiators. That is because, generally, they are too focused on price and products to differentiate. The ones that do use service differentiators generally use 'Explicit claims' as explained earlier. E.g. 'Our service is better'!

You cannot sell service and system differentiators using the traditional features and benefits methods nor can you do so by using explicit claims. To differentiate using services and systems you need to know the impact, of service and system issues, on the prospect's life. You need to understand your prospect's world, not just their buying behaviour.

When you understand the impact of service deficiencies to your customer explain your service and systems benefits using the **GPS model**:

- Generally

- Problem

- Solution & story

Generally

Explain the general situation. What is everyone trying to do? It is good to use the word 'try' here because it implies failure.

Problem

Explain the difficulty that causes problems. This allows you to differentiate without appearing to criticise your competitors.

Solution and story

What does your company do that definitely shows you are different? Tell a story to illustrate your point.

I will work through an example to differentiate between you and a competitor on levels of stock.

Generally 'every company tries to keep the correct stock levels. Everyone knows that if you don't have stock you can't sell it'.

Problem 'the difficulty is there are so many different spare parts that it would need a massive warehouse just to store them'.

Solution 'we definitely understand how annoying it is for a supplier to run out of stock, which is why we have invested in a new stock management system allowing us to fulfil 98% of orders the same day'.

'Last week I had a customer looking for a discontinued part and I managed to find it in another branch and get it to them within one hour'.

Kwik Fit Exhaust Fitters used a great technique to differentiate. They would get your car onto their ramp in order to sell. Their differentiation was often simply that your car was on their ramp.

Let's say your car needs a new exhaust.

You telephone garage A and they tell you the cost for a front box is £180, if you need only the back box it costs £160. If you need a complete system it costs £320. You phone the next garage and they say roughly the same perhaps a little more expensive perhaps a little less.

Then you phone Kwik Fit.

Their salesperson says 'there are different types of exhausts for your model and I don't want to give you wrong advice over the phone. It is unlikely that you would need a complete exhaust anyway. Why don't you bring the car down, I will get my mechanic, Brian, to put it up on a ramp and then we can check exactly what it needs?'

They would then go on to use an alternative close, 'how about today or is tomorrow more suitable for you?'

The people at Kwik Fit know that when they get your car on their ramp they increase their chances of a sale. They will show you the big hole in the exhaust. Then they say 'unfortunately you do need a complete exhaust. They aren't normally a stock item but luckily we just happen to have one in stock. It is actually one that was ordered for a customer who was supposed to come in two days ago but they have been delayed until next week. I can fit it right now for you'! This uses scarcity and reciprocation.

The chances are this sale is no longer price sensitive, it is about convenience and you will even pay a little more. If they had quoted you on the telephone then they would only have got the job based on low price. Their differentiation is not about the exhaust it is about getting your car on their ramp.

There is always a difference between competitors and you. One of the differences is you! You sell your own products you don't sell your competitors products.

We know that the salesperson is a major factor in sales. Your results are directly related to your ability. Of course there are other things that are differentiators such as the location, stock availability, service levels, after-sales care etc. but the major factor that drives your sales is you.

Even your product knowledge is a differentiator. People will pay more to someone with greater product knowledge. That is why specialist shops exist. They may be more expensive but staff should be more knowledgeable than their general competitors.

Improve your own skills and treat customers better and your results will improve.

What differentiators do you need? To decide where to differentiate yourself from the competition, first consider the only two things that sell.

1.) If you can help a prospect grow, i.e. make more profit; or

2.) You can ease a pain they have in their business

Understanding questions help you to identify the pain people have in their business. Start with your prospects and ask what annoys them about the way that your industry works. Don't ask about your company, ask about your market segment – the politeness principle makes it difficult for people to tell you directly about your company.

For example, if you work for a bank then ask 'What does the banking industry do that makes life difficult for you?' Or 'What annoys you about banks?'

If you work for a product supplier you could ask 'what do suppliers do that costs your business money?'

These questions help prospects to evaluate the real cost to their business because of poor service.

When you find out the pain that happens in your industry you need to drill down on that information to build the pain in the customers mind. For example, imagine I asked a customer what annoys them about plumbing suppliers, and they said 'running out of stock items'. I would then ask them what they do when a product is out of stock, what is the impact to their business, how do their customers react when they spend hours looking for another source. Note that I don't ask how often the existing suppliers run out of stock? I am building the pain and if they 'very rarely run out of anything, it only happens occasionally' I have just reduced the pain. The pain is often emotional not logical.

An example of this is a friend who runs his own business. He gets really wound up by his employees wasting time. Even if they aren't wasting time! They only need to look like they are! I reckon he would buy anything if the salesperson was clever enough to tie the benefits of their product to avoiding his employees wasting time!

Find the pain and differentiate your offering by avoiding that pain. If you can't then you need to find ways of helping customers to grow but this is much less successful.

An example of differentiators that would help customers to grow would be a kitchen supplier that could help a home builder to sell more houses because of a revolutionary new design of kitchen.

Given that you now have some differentiation between you and your competitor you should focus on finding at least four of them. Four is the magic number. Always mention at least four differentiators in your summary close.

Studies have shown that if you use less than four differentiators it doesn't create sufficient differentiation. If there are more than four differences between products then comparison is difficult because it is like comparing apples with pears.

ADD-ON SELLING

'Value' and 'Worth' are notoriously difficult to define legally. Let me give you a definition of them that I use on courses.

Value
Value is what you pay or would pay for something. Value is a personal thing. I have photographs, which aren't worth anything, but their value to me is almost priceless.

Worth
Worth is what someone else would pay for it. If I tried to sell my photographs on eBay I would find that they aren't really worth anything!

These definitions are really important as when we are making decisions we react in different ways depending on whether we are making a decision based on:

- An expectancy of gain

- A guaranteed loss

I will explain this difference. Why would someone decide to buy something when they are guaranteed a loss? Remember my definitions of 'value and worth'.

You buy a car for £10000. Its value to you is £10000. You drive it off the forecourt. How much is it worth? How much would someone be prepared to pay you for it? Now you find your car is only worth £7000. You absolutely knew when making your purchase you were faced with a guaranteed loss.

When the car dealer bought your car they perhaps paid the manufacturer £8000. Its value to them is £8000 but it is now worth £10000 because they are hoping to sell it for £10000.

So some purchases are made in the expectation of gain yet others on a guaranteed loss. How we make decisions in these circumstances is very different and well documented. When we are faced with a guaranteed loss we will be more speculative in our decision-making. When we are faced with a prospect of gain we will be much more conservative.

For the same reasons it is easier to sell an upgrade to a retail prospect. Your favourite saying to a retail prospect should be 'for a little more you can get .....'

A trade purchaser is much more conservative. To get these people to make a decision, always show them the Rolls Royce solution first followed by the recommended, more conservative, solution.

Beware of thinking it is only Retail that have a guaranteed loss and Trade a prospect of gain. Personal influences come into play as well. A purchasing manager or engineer may be making a decision to purchase thinking that their career could depend on the outcome. Their purchase may be based on a prospect of personal gain.

When selling accessories decide whether the accessory is an 'enhancement' or a 'protection' product.

Enhancements add to the perceived value of the purchase e.g. an upgraded speaker system for a hi-fi. If you are selling an enhancement to a product the selling of features and benefits must always be sold before the price is discussed.

Protections safeguard the long-term value of the investment e.g. breakdown cover. If you are selling protection the features and benefits must be sold after the sale has been agreed.

NEGOTIATION

The first thing to say about negotiation is that it is much better to avoid negotiation than to engage in it. In particular if you use the techniques described in the section 'Dealing with Peacocks' and 'Understanding Questions' most negotiations should be avoided. Realistically there will still be some people who 'try it on' and also some situations where you may potentially lose business by a small margin.

The first rule in negotiation should therefore be to identify which of the two groups the prospect falls into.

On many courses I get the sense that delegates feel I am completely against negotiation. I am not. I think that before any concessions are given that all other avenues should be exhausted first. Businesses have become so used to giving concessions that they seem take the 'easy' way out. In an hotel recently a foreign work experience lad, who had only been in the country a few months, gave me a discount. The management had already taught him to discount.

To identify which of the two groups the prospect falls into you need to go through the negotiation tree explained in the section 'Dealing with Peacocks':

In this tree I have used 'Price versus Profit', which is a trade model rather than 'Price versus Cost' which is a retail model. The concepts are exactly the same. In a trade sale the prospect may save money on the price and make less profit as happens when they use less expensive products, passing the benefit of this to their prospect, and end up doing a service call because of poor quality products.

<u>After</u> doing this you may need to go through a win/win negotiation, which is the most misunderstood term in selling – win/win negotiations.

How do you conduct negotiations that sell to the emotional decision makers?

I am constantly dismayed by naive attempts to negotiate. In addition I am dismayed by the attitude that concessions are almost inevitable.

Every day in the media someone will tell us: 'The government needs to sit round a table and negotiate.' Or 'so and so are refusing to come to the negotiation table'. It is almost as if negotiation is an inevitable consequence of management and business. What is really meant isn't negotiation, it is about compromise and concessions.

Concessions are a very last step that should only be entered into after all other steps have failed. In reality we play a game where we propose something that we know will be unacceptable so we have something to concede. We hold on to some area (profit or conditions) that we would be prepared to concede in order to get agreement. When we get involved in the game we have this idea that we should meet somewhere in the middle.

Selling is about motivating people to trust you enough to tell you the truth; then helping them discover their real needs as opposed to perceived needs; then helping them to evaluate the cost of failing to meet those needs; and finally proposing a solution from which they will profit while making a sufficient profit for yourself.

Where in selling have we got the notion that we should gain the trust of the prospect in order to abuse and exploit that trust?

My entire strategy with my clients has been to help them understand the need to go in with their best offer first and leave no room for any negotiation. The prospects need to know this is your strategy in the first place. Knowing this they can make decisions with the full knowledge that you have nowhere to go and asking you is pointless. It has been **VERY** successful.

Clients have asked me, 'show me how you would negotiate in this situation?' As if I have some magic wand that I can wave to win a negotiation. I can't help feel that the reason people are looking for a magic solution is that they are playing a win/lose game in the first place. My normal answer to a client is that I would advise selling properly to avoid getting in that situation in the first place!

So what about win/win negotiations? I believe win/win is an outcome, not a negotiation. To achieve this you must understand win/win.

Let me paint a scenario:

You have quoted £100,000 for a contract. The prospect telephones you and asks you to come and see them about the quote.

As an aside, if this does happen you have got the business! No one will ever ask you to come and see them to tell you that you haven't got the business. You need to do follow up calls to find out you haven't got the business. No one likes to be the bearer of bad news. At best you might get an email but rarely personal contact to say you have lost the business.

Before going to see them you sit down with the principal decision makers and decide how low you could go to get the business. You make a decision that you would still make profit at £90k and anything more would be a bonus.

What you don't know is the prospect's side.

The prospect has had quotes ranging from £100k (yours) to £90k from your biggest competitor.

For some reason you may never know, the prospect would prefer to place the business with you. It could be, for example, a credit limit, all eggs in one basket, exposure to single supplier limitations etc. You don't know and the prospect is unlikely to tell you!

This is the prospect that calls and asks you to come and see them. Let me draw that on a grid:

Our Quote	Prospects Best
£100,000	£90,000

Our Lowest	Prospects Maximum
£90,000	£100,000

What would be a win/win agreement?

The vast majority of people I train go for £95k as being a win/win. It isn't. £95k is a compromise agreement. It is a no lose/no lose.

Almost like saying I like Indian food but my wife likes Chinese food so we go to an Italian restaurant!

I have found most people actually go in to a negotiation situation with a compromise in mind. It seems to be the prime objective. I don't have an issue with a compromise solution but it is not an objective. It is a failure to understand win/win. It is also very dangerous as an objective since, if the other party is playing win/lose, and you are looking for a compromise, you will always lose!

A win/win agreement can only happen if both parties win 100%.

To do this you need to step away from a transaction level and start thinking at an objectives level.

I want to sell at £100k to maximise my profit. The prospect wants to buy at £90k to maximise their profit. Therefore a win/win agreement would be one where I make more profit and so do they.

This is not always possible to achieve but it must be the prime objective to achieve win/win. Two ways to achieve it are to:

- Reduce the price and retain or increase your profit

- Retain the price and reduce the customers costs allowing them to achieve the same or more profit despite the higher price

Let me give some examples. You could agree to:

- Substitute alternative products that are equivalents and that you have a higher margin on (preferred products). In doing so you reduce the price to the customer but retain your profit because you have a higher margin on the substituted products.

- Increase the volume so that you can retain or increase profit

- Reduce the price and reduce your costs e.g. direct delivery from a supplier

- Reduce payment terms or even admin costs chasing up payments

- Include a service that is low cost for you and is high value for the prospect

- Package in a way that reduces their handling costs e.g. delivery to individual units

- Find how the customer prices jobs. The example I used earlier when customers price materials by adding a percentage to their cost. If you keep the price and they add 20% they will make more profit than if you reduce the price and they still add 20%.

If you follow these two rules for a win/win negotiation you remove the people who are playing a game. They realise that any concession will be earned rather than given. If you conduct this style of negotiation you will often find prospects coming up with creative solutions as well. They may suggest that part of your service doesn't add value for them and so you can remove it to reduce your costs. Removing a cost allows you to reduce your price and still retain or increase your profit.

How do you stop people from going back to their preferred supplier with your quote? You can't really, your customers do it for you so don't expect others not to. All you can do is minimise the chances of this happening.

You do this by increasing commitment at every stage of the process. Remember I said earlier eight contacts 83% of people buy? At each of these contacts take prospects through the commitment ladder. Increase the level of commitment at each stage.

Some of the levels, from no commitment at all, through to stronger levels:

- Taking a telephone call is a very low level of commitment. It is higher than not taking a call though!

- Agreeing to future contact is almost no commitment

- Accepting a brochure is usually a hidden objection, as is asking for more information

- The length of time on the telephone - slightly higher level of commitment

- Meeting at the prospect's premises - still more

- Meeting at the sales organisation's premises – much more commitment

- Prospect involvement rather than passive interest – higher commitment again

  - Prospects meeting your other customers

  - Prospects preparing requested information

  - Prospects meeting manufacturers

- Meeting additional junior stakeholders i.e. meeting with staff junior to the purchasing contract e.g. the Engineers or Site Managers.

- Meeting additional senior stakeholders i.e. meeting with staff senior to the purchasing contract e.g. the CEO, Logistics Manager, Sales Director. This can often be achieved by matching levels within your own organisation. For example letting your contact know that your CEO wants to be involved in a meeting and would like their CEO involved as well.

- The client agreeing to meet with your stakeholders e.g. your CEO, Logistics Manager, Product Quality Manager etc.

- The client asking to meet your stakeholders e.g. your CEO, Logistics Manager, Product Quality Manager etc.

- Trials of alternative suggestions – high commitment

- Letters of intent – very high

- Low deposits – can be quite low commitment. In Australia people give a low deposit to a homebuilder more to take an option on the house rather than as a commitment to buy it.

- High deposits – extremely high commitment

If you properly work a prospect through the levels of commitment then you will have minimised the chances of being used to 'keep the current supplier honest'. Be wary if the prospect doesn't want to go through them.

After a win/win negotiation if you still need to give a concession then use the phrase:

> 'I don't think I'll be able to match it would you like me to see how close I can get?'

If the prospect agrees and says 'see how close you can get' you rarely need to go beyond meeting them in the middle.

If the prospect says you must match it, or beat it, then this phrase allows you to say, 'I don't think I'll be able to but I will try'. Then the decision is up to your organisation. Before you give a concession I suggest you consider the five concession factors:

1.) Never give something away without asking for something back at the same time. This does a lot less harm to your organisation because prospects feel they have earned the concession rather than been given it.

    This is the only rule you need to remember as the other rules indicate what you can ask for.

2.) Consider their payment history – are they good payers. Remember the cost of cash collection.

3.) Consider their loyalty. Do they buy everything from you or just the products they have to. Loyalty should be rewarded. If the prospect only buys from you when they have to they shouldn't get concessions.

4.) Consider how organised they are. Disorganised people are more expensive to service. Also disorganised people need organised suppliers.

5.) Charge them extra if they are hard to deal with. Aggressive nasty prospects cost your business in terms of staff motivation and retention.

The point of these is only to give concessions to prospects you would rather keep. If you don't mind losing them don't back down. I found that most company's reward their complaining prospects and penalise their best prospects i.e. the loyal non-complaining ones.

⊙BJECTI⊙NS

In handling objections the first thing that needs to be accepted is that I don't have any arguments against your prospect's objections. To take an example if your prospect says your product is 'too expensive because they can buy it cheaper elsewhere'. I have no arguments against this statement. I don't know if they really can get the same product elsewhere. I also don't know how your service compares with 'elsewhere'. I therefore have no knowledge of you, your competitors, your products, your services etc. on which to base any arguments.

In my experience thinking about arguments is the least of your problems. I have never had a salesperson that couldn't think of arguments. The main problem is that the prospects won't accept them.

If the prospects accepted your arguments then the problem would be solved. The prospect would say 'you are too expensive' or 'I can buy it cheaper elsewhere'. You would answer 'yes, but our service is better', or 'our product is better quality'. If they accepted these arguments they would say 'oh is it? Really? Well thank you for that I had better buy from you then – here is my money!'

Unfortunately have you ever noticed the really annoying thing about objections? The prospects don't always accept your arguments. I have even seen examples of prospects appearing to accept the argument 'I agree that yours is better quality but I am still going to buy elsewhere!'

The only thing I can help you with is that I have a method that helps people listen to and be more willing to accept your arguments.

The stages are:

STFU

Empathy Statement

Handle

Close

STFU
That stands for 'Stop Talking!!' (Shut the folder up!)

Let's take the objection 'that's too expensive'.

Imagine someone has just said that to you. What might they mean by this statement?

I can think of:

- The product isn't worth the price

- There is another identical product that is less expensive

- It isn't worth that much more than another inferior product

- It is a higher cost than they expected

- They can't afford it

- It is too good quality e.g. a Rolls Royce is too expensive for me

- Someone told them they should pay less than that amount

- It could be the start of a negotiation strategy

- They don't like it

Before you even attempt to handle the objection you should find out what they mean by 'too expensive'.

Note here that the most natural thing here would be to ask them 'Why do you think it is too expensive?' or 'What makes you say that?' or 'How come?' or even 'compared to what?'

These aren't brilliant things to do though. All of them involve you forcing the prospect to take a stand and because they don't want to be proved wrong you actually make it harder for them to accept your arguments.

The first thing you need to do is to use the one-second rule. Stay silent for one second, which gives the signal that you are interested in their objection and that you are looking for some further clarification. If you stay silent the prospect will say something more and the second thing they say will be more accurate than the first.

So the prospect may say 'That is too expensive ..... err I can buy it cheaper elsewhere'.

The one-second rule is a perfect strategy here. That is because of a concept known as 'Preferred' responses and 'Non Preferred' responses.

When people give you a preferred response they do not feel the need to explain. When people give you a non-preferred response they **always** feel the need to explain.

For example, if you ask someone if they would like a cup of tea. People will be able to say 'yes please' without giving an explanation. If they want to say 'No' that is a non-preferred response and they will always feel the need to explain.

They will say things such as:

'No thanks, I've just had one'

'No thanks, I'm in a hurry'

'No thanks, I don't like tea'

All objections are, by definition, 'non preferred' responses.

If a prospect says 'that's too expensive' and you leave them a one-second gap they will explain and tell you exactly what they mean.

Only when you have an explanation and a full understanding of the objection can you hope to handle it.

This takes us on to the next stage:

Empathy Statements

The prospect's expectations are critical at this stage. Imagine if you were being sold a chair and you said to the salesperson that you 'thought the chair was too expensive ..... it isn't good quality'. What would you expect the salesperson to do? Most of us would expect the salesperson to show the quality of the manufacture and show us how we are wrong. In essence we expect salespeople to argue with us!

Because of this expectation we are resistant to any arguments from the salesperson at this time.

If you want people to listen to your arguments you need to construct an empathy statement. An empathy statement **cannot** include the words 'but', 'however' or 'although' at any time. Nor can they include the phrase 'on the other hand' or similar. These are arguments not empathy statements.

The prospect will **always** agree with an Empathy statement. If they don't then you have constructed an argument, not an empathy statement.

The third stage of handling objections is:

Handle

When handling use the phrase:

'and what we need to do is ..... don't we?'

You can vary the language but always end with a positive followed by a negative such as 'do need to do - don't we', should do -shouldn't we', could do - couldn't we' etc.

For example for the objection 'I can buy it cheaper elsewhere' the empathy statement and move to handling may be 'Yes and if I could get the same thing cheaper elsewhere I would buy it there as well and what we need to do is to check it is the same thing for you don't we?'

Some examples of empathy statements and links to handling objections may be:

Objection
'The product isn't worth the price'

Empathy Statement and link to handling phase
'Yes it is a lot of money isn't it, and what we need to do is look at all the features to see whether it is the correct product for you, don't we!'

Objection
'There is another product that is less expensive'

Empathy Statement and link to handling phase
'Yes I am sure there are. There are many cheaper products available in the market place and if I could get exactly the same thing cheaper elsewhere I would buy it as well and what we need to do is look and check that it is exactly the same, don't we!'

Objection
'It isn't worth that much more than another similar product'

Empathy Statement and link to handling phase
'They look very similar don't they and what we should to do is have a look at the differences and see if they are worth paying the extra for shouldn't we!'

Objection
'I can't afford it'

Empathy Statement and link to handling phase
'We all have budget constrains don't we and what we need to do is make sure that you have the best value solution isn't it!'

Objection
'It could be the start of a negotiation strategy i.e. is that your best price?'

Empathy Statement and link to handling phase

'Yes I want to make it as attractive as possible for you and we should investigate any suggestions you may have to make our proposal as attractive as possible to you, shouldn't we!'

Note the empathy statements end on an exclamation mark not a question mark. These are said as statements not questions. The point of them is to move the customer from the objection to the handling phase with the minimum resistance.

OK now you get to bring your superior knowledge of the product, competitors and your service etc. into play.

Some strategies for handling objections are:

Break it to the ridiculous

Breaking to the ridiculous involves reducing figures to a small insignificant amount.

For example you can consider things:

- Compared to other quotes so a contract worth $50k may be only $3k more expensive.

- On a hourly basis – a bath costing $1000 costs less than $0.20c per day over the 15 year lifetime of a bath

- On a profit level – a contract worth $10k at 21% GP is worth a gross profit of $2100

- On a per delivery basis – if the above contract involved 10 deliveries it would be a GP of just $210 per delivery

- Over time – if the above contract were over one year you could reduce it to gross profit of $40 per week

Imagine you are buying a hi-fi. The one you want costs £500 but you feel that is too expensive. Breaking it to the ridiculous involves handling the objection using the smallest amount possible.

For example with a £500 hi-fi the alternative would be to get one that is slightly lower quality that would cost, say £400.

What we are talking about is a difference of £100.

The average hi-fi today probably lasts for 10 years (I have had my hi-fi for longer than that).

We are now talking about £10 a year or less than £1 per month. That is less than 25p per week or about 3p per day.

Is it worth paying an extra 3p per day to get exactly what you want?

Comparison theory

Always compare the difference rather than the full price. For example instead of talking about your price being £1000 focus on the difference between your price and the competitors price. So we are only £60 dearer on a product that costs £1000. Or better still we are only 6% out on a product that costs £1000.

Use percentages when the amount is small and amounts when the percentages are small. For example if the price is £20 a discount of £0.50 doesn't sound much so use nearly 3%. If you are talking about £10,000 a £300 discount may sound better.

COMPLAINTS

Generally businesses should have a good product returns policy. Accept all returns, no questions asked and give a full refund. Make it easy for the prospect and never charge restocking fees. When a businessman gets used to buying more than they need and returning the excess you have a customer for life.

Calculate how much your credit returns cost you. Remember to work out the net cost. For example, let's say you take back a product you sold last month for £1000. You need to consider:

- How much did you pay for it?

- How much can you resell it for?

- How quickly will you resell it?

- You have had the customer's money for a month!

- Your supplier credit terms.

- You didn't risk losing or damaging it in that month.

In most cases people look at the gross amount refunded on returns and consider that as a loss to the business. Most credit returns cost much less than you think.

Now consider how many additional sales you could achieve if you remove the risk of making a wrong purchase.

For example I won't use Trainline in the UK. The reason for this is that their website is complex and it defaults to different dates when you hit 'search again'. I have made too many errors in the past, which they wouldn't correct! Any savings I may achieve are wiped out by my occasional error and so it doesn't pay me to use them despite their discounted prices.

From a salesperson point of view the best question to ask customers is 'I am really sorry this has happened and I would like to fix it for you, what would you like me to do to fix it?'

There seems to be a lot of fear in doing this but there shouldn't be. The statistics:

20% of customers simply want an apology and to get the problem fixed.

30% want less than you would be prepared to do to fix it.

30% want about the same as you are prepared to do to fix it.

Only 20% want more than you are prepared to do to fix it.

Asking the question above doesn't change the percentages it merely identifies the 20% you have a problem with.

All complaints have to be fixed!

How many times has your company been taken to court?

More statistics, 77% of customers whose complaint has been fixed immediately, by the first person they first speak to, are very satisfied. This drops to 61% if it is the second person they speak to and so on down the line until if the complaint is fixed by senior management the figure is almost zero.

Complaints solved by senior management usually involve giving more than the customer originally wanted. This means the process of getting them to escalate the complaint gets them so angry they also increase their demands.

The message is clear – fix complaints quickly!

CLOSING

The most overrated skill. The best sales happen when you have done your job well and the prospect asks how quickly you can implement your proposal. I love it when a prospect says 'I need that now, how quickly can you get it here!'

I would define a close as a call to action. It may be that you are closing for a first or subsequent meeting, or closing for an order.

Techniques are not as successful as doing a proper job. If you haven't done your job well the techniques won't rescue you. The best salespeople don't use many different closing techniques they get the prospect so excited by their proposition that the prospect closes them. The close for great salespeople becomes a natural flowing part of going to the next stage.

Some people are hesitant about the call to action (it is where they may experience rejection) and so the following may help.

I do believe that the ability to stay silent after any close is critical. It is often said the first person that speaks after a close owns the product. What is meant is, if the prospect speaks first they will buy it, if the salesperson speaks first, they won't. I am sure this isn't literally true but it is a good guide.

Summary

The summary close is the most effective method of closing.

The summary close means you summarise the four differentiators you have identified and then ask for the business.

For example, 'you are getting the model with the 4mm thicker metal which will last longer. The four-year guarantee to protect you and it has the four settings so you can tackle a variety of jobs. It also comes in the colour you were looking for, shall we go ahead with the order?'

Summarise the benefits, ask for the order, and then stay silent.

Direct

A direct close is a direct closed question e.g. 'do you want to go ahead?'

Trial

Good for 'Owls' and 'Doves'. This is a question about their thoughts e.g. 'how useful do you think having that facility would be for your business?'

Alternative

This offers the option between two positive outcomes rather than deciding yes or no e.g. 'do you want it in red or blue?'

Assumptive

This is also a good close for 'Doves'. You assume you are getting the business and don't actually ask them. Go ahead with ordering for them and then they have to stop you.

Minor Issue

Usually used as, or in conjunction with, an Assumptive close. This is where you ask a question about something insignificant. When they answer this question it is clear they are going ahead e.g. 'we only deliver to your area on Wednesday, is this coming Wednesday OK for you?'

The important thing about the Assumptive and the Minor issue closes is you must never ask them if they are going ahead. For example I was coaching a salesman who used a minor issue close. He said 'what is the address for delivery?' The prospect told him the address and he responded 'so you want to go ahead then?' Sorry ..... wrong!!

Prescription (also called the Duke of Wellington or Winston Churchill)

This has to be the worst close I have ever been taught and if any salesperson tried this on me they would be sent on their merry way with a small insect in their listening apparatus!

The prescription close is where you help someone by saying 'You know when Churchill had a decision to make he would list all the pros and cons on a piece of paper'.

Then you would help the prospect to list all the pros for buying the product.

When it comes to considering the cons over buying, you leave them for a few minutes thinking about the cons. When they have difficulty you help them by adding 'the price' to the cons.

At the end you are supposed to have a long list of pros and a small list of cons. If you are selling to me you are more likely to feel cold (being back in the great outdoors - outside my place of business!!)

I am sure many people use this very successfully but not on me!

ATTITUDE

When training I ask groups to imagine I have just been promoted to Sales Director for their company. I have gathered together this group of expert salespeople and asked them for help. My task is to increase sales. I wouldn't discount anything on the basis of limited budgets. All ideas would be considered. I pose the question 'What could you do to increase sales?'

The list usually includes the following:

Ways to increase sales:

- More advertising (this almost always comes first)

- TV advertising

- Newspaper and magazines

- Trade shows and publications

- Sponsorship

- New product lines

- Improve existing products

- Increase stock

- Increase number of salespeople

- Increase number of locations

- Take over the competition (unlimited budget remember)

- Better cars for salespeople

- Incentives

- More training (I like to end on a high note!)

I would like to give my ideas on an original model by Dr Stephen Covey in his great book, The Seven Habits of Highly Effective People.

There are things that 'Concern' us and we don't feel we have any influence over.

Some things we can 'Influence' but we cannot control.

And we have 100% control over our own attitude and behaviour.

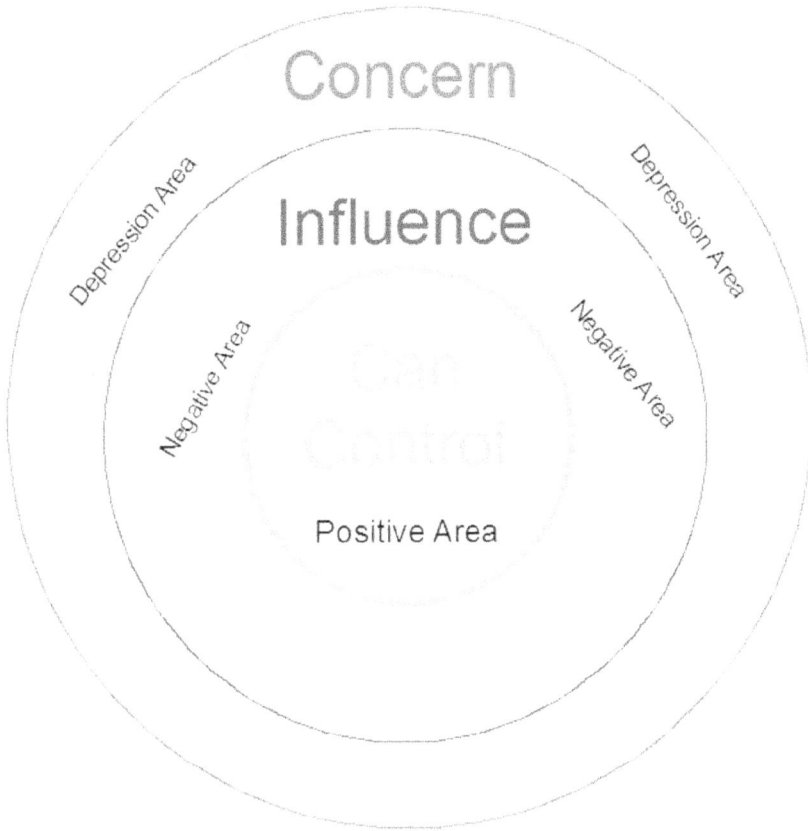

He calls this idea the Circles of Concern.

For example:

I am concerned about death but I have no influence over it. I have some influence (perhaps) over when it may happen but I know it will happen; I have no influence over whether it will happen.

I have some influence over my health but I cannot control my health because of the possibility of disease etc.

I can control what I eat, how much exercise I do etc. I only control my own attitude and behaviour.

Notice that these are personal levels. For example, I am concerned about world poverty and I feel I have no influence over it. I can donate to charity but I don't think that influences world poverty. What the charity chooses to do with my donation may have some small influence over world poverty. My influence is so negligible that I consider it to be in my area of concern.

For the singer Bono, he would undoubtedly consider world poverty to be within his sphere of influence. He can speak to Barack Obama and have a meeting to discuss world poverty. He definitely thinks he has some influence there otherwise he wouldn't keep doing the things he does.

In his book Stephen Covey gives some great tips using this model. I have noticed something else about the model.

Generally when you speak with someone who is depressed or addicted they seem to explain by giving reasons that they see as concern issues while others see them as control issues. When someone suffers from depression they seem to feel that there are some things they cannot for whatever reason control. For example, a gambling addict will say that they are unable to control whether they bet on something. They 'have' to do it. For me the decision to gamble is an easy decision and completely within my area of control.

I should say here that I am not attacking people with depression or addictions. I don't understand depression and I have never suffered from it so I am not in a position to judge those people who do suffer from it. They have my sympathy. I don't know how or why it happens; it just seems to me that it does. I don't have any advice on how to stop it happening either.

I do remember a David Attenborough documentary that suggested that addiction is a genetic disorder, so I am not having a go!

When I talk to negative, cynical people I feel they focus on others who are in their area of influence. It is always the fault of the bosses, other staff, prospects etc. In my experience there is one person that very few cynics blame for their situation.

When I talk with positive and successful people they all seem to have one thing in common. They all focus all of their efforts on what they can control. Their thinking seems to be: 'Yes, it has happened, now what can we do about it?'

Look back at the list of answers to the question: 'What could **YOU** do to increase sales?' This time I have emphasised the key word. The previous list is really a combination of Concern and Influence issues.

To increase sales I can:

- Pick up the phone more times

- Work harder

- See more people

- Ask all of them to buy

- Learn about my own product

- Support my colleagues

- Learn about selling

- Read books about selling - you have made a good start, and I like to end on a high note!

I often get people claiming that they have some influence over things I see as concern issues. For example, people say they have some influence over the competition because 'if we reduce our prices then they will have to reduce theirs.' If it was our influence that caused that then it should also work in reverse. If we put up our prices would they have to increase theirs?

With advertising I also get people saying they can input to the marketing department and influence them. It will never cease to amaze me why people with absolutely no expertise in marketing think they know better than someone with a degree in the subject and who has studied it for years.

My attitude is that I should leave them to do their job to the best of their ability while I focus on doing my job to the best of mine. They deserve my support, not my criticism!

If you can influence your marketing department, give them a call; use all your influence; if nothing changes then you didn't have influence! It is in your area of concern, forget it, get on with life and focus on doing the best job that you can.

To see the power in this model, who will be more effective and happier? The person that complains about the lack of advertising or the one that focuses on their prospect development?

If you want to be successful read and reread this book. Selling is simple but it isn't easy. I have spent years developing these techniques they can't be perfected in a day.

Good luck, although luck has nothing to do with it, and if you implement everything contained in this book it will all be 'Plain Selling'.

SUMMARY

Section 1

Decision-making is emotional not logical and selling is not a perfect science. There is no 'right' way to sell. Develop your own style. Take what works for you and ditch what doesn't.

Much sales training has been based on logical thinking and therefore some selling myths have arisen.

Selling is about:

1.) Avoiding objections

2.) Handling them if you fail to avoid them

Section 2

Some psychological factors affect us all:

- Confirmation Bias - price isn't as important as most salespeople think

- We use shortcuts to facilitate decision making

  - Authority - we overemphasise the importance of uniforms and experts

  - Conformity - we go in entrances and leave by exits

- Consistency - we don't want to be seen as inconsistent. Affluent one minute then skinflint the next

- Peer Pressure - we are more likely to behave like our peer group

- Reciprocation - 'no obligation' makes people feel obliged

- People don't like to be proved wrong – they defend their stance

- Scarcity - increases desirability

- Liking - similarities help people to trust us

- Comparison Theory - £220 seems less if £300 was mentioned immediately before

- Optimists and Pessimists - sell to them differently

- We have a need for praise and will actively seek it

- Buying Motivators

  - Habit - the most powerful

  - Emotion - of these fear and greed are the most powerful

    - Avoiding pain is more motivational than going for pleasure

  - Logic - is the least powerful motivator

- Buyer's remorse - after purchasing we wonder if we have done the right thing

- Regret

- Missing out in a small way is worse that completely failing

- Changing and failing hurts more than sticking and failing

- Implied & Explicit statements - the power of implied statements and the danger of explicit claims

- Labels we give customers and how they affect our relationships

- Choice - 'Paralysis by choice'

- The six most important words in selling

  - Why - only use in positive situations

  - Because - makes us sound like an expert and gives us a reason to do something

  - But - avoid it if you can substitute 'and'

  - Try doesn't differentiate - Definitely does

  - Risk - people would generally prefer to avoid taking risks

- Deal with the behaviour

  - Eagles - ask future questions

  - Owls - ask past, factual then past opinion questions

  - Doves - close them or use them - use reciprocation

  - Peacocks - use the negotiation tree

- Decision influencers

  - Economic buyer -

    - Real motivator - convenience

    - Perceived motivator - price

    - Not motivated by features

  - Technical buyer

    - Real motivator - convenience

    - Perceived motivator - features

    - Not motivated by price

  - User buyer

    - Real motivator - convenience

    - Perceived motivator - price or benefits

    - Not motivated by price

- Optimists and pessimists needs are different

- Relationship selling - add value in business first

- Ambience - appropriate music and uniforms

- The introduction and approach

- Questioning - using understanding questions to identify pain

- Proposing solutions - using four differentiators

- Add-on selling - easy in retail but go for conservative options in B2B selling

  - Negotiation - win/win isn't compromise

    - Reduce price but retain profit

    - Maintain price but reduce customers costs

  - Differentiate

    - Products using **FAB** model

    - Features - facts

    - Advantages - explanation of features

    - Benefits - opinions on what it does for the customer

    - Services using **GPS** model

    - General situation

    - Problem that makes this difficult

    - Solution and story

  - Objections process

    - STFU - one second silence rule

- Empathy statement - gets 100% agreement

- Handle

- Complaints - solve the problem first time

- Closing techniques

  - Summary close - summarise 4 differentiators

  - Direct - ask for the order

  - Trial - test the water often

  - Alternative between two positive choices

  - Assumptive - assume the order

  - Minor issue - often used with an assumptive close

- Attitude

  - Control - the most successful people focus entirely on control issues

  - Influence

  - Concern

ACKNOWLEDGEMENTS

Grateful thanks to my wife Julie for her diligent proof reading! It makes it so much better when someone else reads through.

Thanks also to Paul Richardson for his creative illustrations.

And to everyone else who knows me! You have contributed to my inspiration.